kidunique

 *Helping Kids Discover Who They Are*

Dan Webster

with Tony Schwartz and Chris Trethewey

KidUnique
Helping Kids Discover Who They Are

Credits
Authors: Dan Webster, Tony Schwartz, Chris Tretheway
Executive Developer: Nadim Najm
Chief Creative Officer: Joani Schultz
Editor: Rob Cunningham
Cover Art Director: Troy Murphy
Designers: Troy Murphy and Riley Hall
Production Manager: DeAnne Lear

ISBN 978-0-7644-6682-3

10 9 8 7 6 5 4 3 2 1   20 19 18 17 16 15 14 13 12 11

Printed in the United States of America.

This book is dedicated to three young men whom I love and who call me "Dad." It continues to be my great honor to encourage them to live their extraordinary lives.

To my sons I say, "Go big or don't go at all."

Luke—You are one of the hardest workers I have ever known. Keep showing up and doing what you do. You have great aesthetic instincts—trust them. You have a big heart. Keep letting it be seen by your dear wife Whitney and others you love. You are content when most are restless. Enjoy the core of life. You are a real and non-judgmental friend—do not change. You enjoy life deeply when others complain. Stay grateful. And you are one of the toughest men I have ever known so keep knocking down every challenge.

Landan—You have a genius way of seeing life—trust your instincts. You have an amazing work ethic. Keep working hard and you will get the life you always wanted. You have never backed down from any big challenge yet. Stay brave and continue killing the giants. You are a deep and loyal friend—fearlessly love from your heart. Stay on the dance floor. Keep hearing the music. You refuse to settle. Keep the bar high. And keep loving excellence. Make your contribution beautiful.

Logan—You enjoy life. Keep living the dream. You are smart—do not apologize for that. You are romantic. Keep letting your heart show. You are a leader—push the right agenda forward. You are secure and instinctive—follow your gut. You are always the first one off the cliff. Be wise in the risks you take. You are trustworthy. Never underestimate the power of trust. And you have a heart for God. Keep listening and following.

Gratitudes

I am not sure how to say thanks to all those who have made a significant contribution to my life, and by doing so, to this project. I learned a long time ago a person can only give what he has received, and I have received much from many.

Without sounding too corny, I want to begin by thanking my mom and dad. My dad passed in May of 1989, but I know he would be proud. Every younger man needs the admiration of an older man, and I miss his love and affirmation. Others have stepped in and are gifting me with light and encouragement, but a dad's voice is hard to replace. My mom's belief in me has never wavered. For Dave and Mona Webster I am grateful.

In 1995 I met Tom Paterson. Like so many others, Tom has dramatically impacted my life. He guided me through his amazing LifePlanning process into my second half. Tom is a true Yoda. I have never met anyone quite like him. A brilliant process thinker and sage, he not only taught me the value and potential of every human being, he models it every day. To be around Tom is to be valued. Everyone is extraordinary to Tom. I love that about him. He is a man of great sorrow and insight. Maybe one does not come without the other. Thanks, Tom, for guiding the way.

There are many others who read this manuscript and gave me real-world feedback on my lofty ideas. They brought me down to earth and made the content better. A special thanks goes out to my beloved wife Judy, Julian Petzold, Linda Lindquist-Bishop, Logan Webster, and Laura Schulenburg. Troy Murphy is a design genius and did the layout of the book. Way to go, stud! Jim Raymond's artistic eye and photos selection were critical. De Jackson did the heavy lifting on the editing side of things. U R the best! So many others told me not to quit on the book and that my thoughts mattered. To Joe Horness, Lamont Moon, Lance Murdock, Gus Gustafson, Brian and Mary Lubinski, Rob and Becky Englin, Tim Lowe, Rohn Ritzema, Dave and Lori Chow, Denny and Scoob Ellens, Jim and Lynn Eickhoff, and so many others—I bless you for your ongoing friendship, belief, and support.

Then there are Tony Schwartz and Chris Trethewey—two of the finest youth workers in America. They are even finer husbands, fathers, and men. Without their encouragement and expertise this project would never have seen paper. Tony is truly "all that" and never met a moment that is too big for him. I love this about him. Chris is a man of deep courage. He knows what it is like to love and lose a child. His passion for fathering inspires me, and his heart is as big as a Vegas jackpot. I am humbled that these men took the challenge of putting together the 31-Day Experience. Like me, this book would not be the same without them.

One last group I must thank is all my LifePlan™ friends. Over the last 18 months I have had the privilege of facilitating LifePlans for many wonderful and gifted people. They endured, and actually welcomed, interruptions when I talked about the content of this book as it relates to life process. As a result I received incredible input and sage advice. So, thanks to Jim, Ben, Guy, Molly, Lori, Manuel, Carter, Keith, Tim, Tom and Sheri, Aric, Dan, and Laura. To God be the glory.

The Authors

Dan Webster is an author, teacher, communicator, mentor, and founder of Authentic Leadership, Inc. Dan's passion is to train and inspire leaders to live authentic lives of great impact. Dan has 30+ years of experience working with leaders from all walks of life: marketplace leaders, teachers, youth workers, pastors, and leaders of nonprofit organizations. He has worked in education, probation, and on the staff of two of the largest and most influential churches in America. Dan has been a visiting professor at graduate schools in Illinois, South Dakota, and Canada. Dan is captivated with both understanding and helping people grow and develop. Dan was born in the Midwest, has been married to Judy for 36 years, and has three grown sons (and a beautiful daughter-in-law). He currently resides in Holland, Michigan.
authenticleadershipinc.com

Tony Schwartz understands student ministry. When he was a sophomore in high school, some friends invited him to check out an awesome student ministry and it changed the direction of his life. Those experiences, and the influence of some great leadership, helped Tony find Christ. Building teams to create thriving student ministry, influential student leaders, and difference-making friendships are passions that drive him. Tony is the director of the Element Junior High Ministry at Central Christian Church in Henderson, Nevada. He is a graduate of Wheaton College and the Lake Forest Graduate School of Management. Tony and Lisa have been married for 19 years and have two strikingly handsome sons, Robby and Riley, and one little girl named Ellie, who is pretty beyond reasonable standards.
centralchristian.com/henderson/students/

Chris Trethewey is a member of the Executive Team at Central Christian Church, where thousands of people attend campuses each weekend, along with a global community who attend online. Chris has spent over 15 years in youth ministry, where his passion for students to thrive in their faith continues to be a focus. He is passionate about the family and is a sought after speaker at both student and family events. He and his wife, Kim, have two beautiful and creative daughters, Kiara and Claire.
centralchristian.com/henderson/students/

Contents

WHAT KIDS NEED MOST

Introduction
Are You Serious?

*Point your kids in the right direction—
when they're old they won't be lost.*

Proverbs 22:6 The Message

"...I have written your name on the palms of my hands."

Isaiah 49:16

"You'll never amount to anything. You are an ugly b#$%*, a slut, and you will never be successful."

What we are up against

Beth was a sophomore in high school when I first met her. She was invited to the student ministry I led. She was bright and gifted in the arts. She also carried a crippling backpack of hurt that put her future well-being in jeopardy. Her parents were not healthy people. Her mom was miserable and afraid to leave the house. Her dad was mean and hated his life. Often when a man does not have the courage to face and fix his life, he turns his pain on others. In this case both parents' personal frustration cascaded onto Beth. Unable to manage his misery, Beth's dad would say to her as she left for school in the morning, *"You'll never amount to anything. You are an ugly b#$%*, a slut, and you will never be successful."* I know, I cannot believe it either. But these are the words he spoke. They stuck to Beth's soul like pine sap.

The unrelenting accumulation of these words fueled a goal in Beth to one day prove her father wrong. Her longing was to become wildly successful in a career. On the surface there is nothing wrong with that goal. Achieving something in life is a good thing. But her goal was not fueled by healthy motivations like desiring to honor God or serving the world with her gift. It was driven by an abiding bitterness toward her dad. Her goal was to one day stand at her father's deathbed, raise her middle finger, and say, *"Screw you dad, you're wrong, I am successful. Now go to hell, you bastard."*

What if Beth's parents had been more positive and encouraging? What if her dad had told her every now and then that she was beautiful, that she mattered? The vision of this book is just that: Kids matter. Its goal is to rally parents, teachers, coaches, youth workers, and anyone else who cares about a kid to get off the sidelines and into the discovery game. They can do it by expressing a seriously ridiculous kind of love that says...*you matter, you have gifts and talents to share with the world, you have a future of hope and meaning...and I will walk with you for a season to help you discover who you are.* What might that look like? How does such a thing happen? Let me paint a picture.

Inspiration from gym class

When it comes to physical education, the Naperville (Illinois) School District 203 has it right.[1] In a day when a third of U.S. schoolchildren are overweight, 90 percent of Naperville District 203 kids are fit. Not only are they fit, these students score consistently higher than the national average on tests in math and science. How can this be? Is there something in the water, or what?

What is happening in Naperville can be traced back to a visionary junior high physical education teacher who came across a newspaper article in 1990 reporting that the health of U.S. children was declining. This concerned and innovative coach began a new movement: the New P.E. The New P.E. has shifted the emphasis in physical education from sports and skill to effort and fitness. Along the way he discovered that when exercise is done right, it dramatically affects a kid on many levels, especially the ability to learn.

This New P.E. curriculum has been designed to teach kids the principles, practice, and importance of fitness. Every school in Naperville District 203 uses a TriFit assessment. This is a computerized health diagnostic system administered to kids beginning in fifth grade. It gives young students targets for heart rate, blood pressure, body fat, and the rest. It is a proven method of motivating kids to stay fit. One of the physical education teachers in the school district put it this way: It's his job to make kids know all of the things they need to know to keep themselves fit.

What is really compelling about this program is that at graduation, students are handed a 14-page health assessment document that chronicles their health history from fifth grade to graduation. It combines fitness scores with other factors like blood pressure and cholesterol levels, and tracks lifestyle and family history surveys. One researcher said it is an astonishingly comprehensive document by any professional health standard, one that an 18-year-old can have in hand when stepping into adult life. At 18, he or she walks out of high school with a diploma and a 14-page document that acts as a guide to the future, offering direction on how to stay fit and keep a brain nimble. How cool is that? Nice job, Naperville!

The bigger picture

As much as I admire what these schools are doing, how much more life-affecting would it be if a student could walk out of junior high or high school with a different type of document? Not one that chronicles their health history, but one that tracks a history of gifts, talents, and uniqueness. This one would be lovingly prepared by an adult who is crazy about them. It contains the truth of who a kid is at his or her core. It would be the fruit of dozens of conversations with a kid. The goal is for a kid to walk out of high school and into adult life with a compilation of insights gathered over the years that uncovers the very essence of who they are. The document would contain precious truths discovered as a kid bumps into life, day in and day out. It would reveal who this kid is—and who he or she isn't.

Maybe it would take the form of a letter or a journal that records thoughts and insights over a period of time. Or maybe it takes the form of this book that will be cluttered with scribbled thoughts and insights after you do the *31-Day Experience.*

For Parker J. Palmer it will take the form of a letter he is preparing for his granddaughter, whom he greatly loves.

> In those early days of my granddaughter's life, I began observing the inclinations and proclivities that were planted in her at birth. I noticed, and I still notice, what she likes and dislikes, what she is drawn toward and repelled by, how she moves, what she does, what she says.
>
> I'm gathering observations in a letter. When my granddaughter reaches her late teens or early 20s, I will make sure that my letter finds its way to her, with a preface something like this: *"Here is a sketch of who you were from your earliest days in this world. It is not a definitive picture—only you can draw that. But it*

was sketched by a person who loves you very much. Perhaps these notes will help you do sooner something your grandfather did only later: remember who you were when you first arrived and reclaim the gift of true self." 2

Can you feel the power a letter like that could have? How precious will that letter be to her in the coming years? Creating such a letter is a **sacred task**3 that will call for our best effort and engagement. To observe inclinations and proclivities, likes and dislikes, what kids are drawn to and repulsed by, how they move, what they do, what they say, and what their gifts and talents are will require the best of our love, patience, thought, and focus. But ask yourself: What task is more important?

College and professional athletes spend long hours dissecting opposing teams to increase their chances of winning. Smart businesspeople spend weeks or months investigating potential mergers to raise the probabilities of success in a future venture. Isn't it wise to invest the needed time and energy into the all-important task of helping kids discover who they are so they can **win in life**4?

Parents, youth workers, and teachers are all concerned for the mental, emotional, physical, and spiritual development of the young. This book equips those entrusted with the development of the next generation to go one step further and help kids begin to solve the mystery of "me." Every life is a mystery waiting to be uncovered, not a mistake needing to be corrected. Entering adulthood with both a foundation of loving interaction with an adult and clarity addressing who they are (the "true self" as Palmer mentions) is priceless. And investing the needed time and energy to help them win in life is just plain smart.

This book is for anyone who wants to impact the lives of kids, but most of the time I will be writing as though speaking to parents. "Kid" is a word I will use throughout this book to describe the focus of our attention. Your "kid" may be your own child or a student you teach, coach, or lead in a small group. Maybe he or she is a relative who has had a tough go of it, so

"Every life is a mystery waiting to be uncovered, not a mistake needing to be corrected."

you are stepping in to help. As far as age goes, "kid" can refer to children in elementary school or students in college. A good friend coaches linebackers at a Division 1 university and he calls his players "kids." Obviously, the application of all the principles shared here will have to be adjusted based on age. We will talk more about that later, and clear direction will be given in the *31-Day Experience*.

The payoff

When it is all said and done, we want a kid who is engaged by a KidUnique adult to:

- feel loved and know they matter because someone paid attention to them.

- have a boost in self-esteem as each is reminded he or she is a miracle, not just a mess.

- have an increased belief in self and respect for others.

- discover their talents and strengths by trying new things.

- be closer to understanding their true selves and be OK with that.

- learn to both appreciate and live into their true selves.

- grow by going for new adventures and opportunities.

- hear words identifying "what's right" instead of only "what's wrong."

- learn to hear the voice of God and receive the help of God, because someone prays for them daily.

For these objectives to be reached, we must learn how to develop a nurturing relationship with a kid. We nurture business deals, investments, and even our gardens. KidUnique is about nurturing a living, breathing human being, adored and made by God.

Nurturing a kid is encouraging him or her to grow, develop, thrive, and be successful. It builds **value**[5] into them. How do kids learn they have value? Kids learn this core truth by how you treat them, day in and day out. Your words and deeds expose what you believe about them. When you listen, cheer for, hope the best for, pray for, see, and love, you are nurturing a kid and clearly saying he or she has value. Kids see their value in our eyes, they hear it in our words, and they feel it in our actions. It seems like every recently published study I read stresses the transforming power of nurturing relationships with those who are young.[6]

I can understand why this is true. These studies tell us that the majority of today's teenagers are angry and hurt because few adults are interested enough to really get to know them. They feel abandoned as a group and left to raise themselves.[7] Kids today are longing for older, trustworthy adults who will listen, care, and just be around occasionally. A friend recently shared with me how life impacting it was for him when an adult stepped toward him in high school. He said, *"He didn't want anything or judge me in the way my parents and others did. He simply cared about me as a person and continually expressed that he believed in me. Every time I heard that I felt great about myself."*

Nothing is more powerful than a loving relationship where an older person values a kid by expressing interest in his or her life. Every person needs and longs for the admiration of someone older and wiser. KidUnique brings us face-to-face with young people. We get the privilege of **reflecting God's heart**[8] to them as we engage their world and search for the core of who God has made them to be.

KidUnique teaches adults (and students, too, we hope) the principles, practice, and importance of sorting a kid out and helping him or her live life from God's plan. You will be able to **sort a kid out**[9] as you track insights gleaned by paying attention to his or her interaction with life. These insights get collected, discussed, and evaluated for validity. As you read this book, record important discoveries on the pages or purchase a special journal to track your insights concerning your kid.

In the end, each kid benefits by taking a huge step forward in getting a clear view of who he or she is, as well as strengths and passions. This becomes a powerful force guiding kids into what can feel like a very tumultuous future. It is our job to help kids move into the future from a position of strength, not weakness—confidence, not fear.

You may be thinking...are you serious? How in the world will I ever pull this off? Do not panic. The four-window model below will help create a framework to guide you through the core principles necessary to discover who a kid is and help you collect insights about the kid you love. Throughout this book you will get your arms around the four-window model, and then in the back of the book there is a practical and transformational *31-Day Experience* that applies these four concepts.

The four windows

Let me introduce the four-window model. These windows unleash a powerful force for discovery in the way we see kids. Every window is a compelling lens through which we watch a kid grow. As you actively look through and understand the four windows, they will alter the relational compass in your brain as to how you relate to kids in the future.

Window One:

OBSERVATION...the power of "seeing" kids.

We track, assess, and confirm insights.

Window Two:

EXPLORATION...the power of inspiring kids to learn about themselves by trying new opportunities and adventures.

We discuss these and identify interests and strengths.

Window Three:

AFFIRMATION...the power of identifying and telling a kid what's right with him or her.

We see it and say it.

Window Four:

REVELATION...the power of listening for God's whispers that touch the identity and calling of a kid.

We pray for our kids and listen for the "heavenly messengers."

OBSERVATION   EXPLORATION

AFFIRMATION   REVELATION

These four windows are different lenses to peer into each moment of the day. They make the expression of our love an action. They position us around a kid so that we can gain perspective. *Observation* will put us right in front of a kid looking straight on and seeing what we can see. *Exploration* puts us right next to a kid as we inspire discovery and help process reactions. *Affirmation* puts us behind a kid speaking encouragement and reminding what's right with him or her. *Revelation* puts us on our knees at the feet of a kid as we earnestly ask God for insight and help.

I hope the vision of what can happen is getting clearer. An adult who is engaged in KidUnique turns loose the power of the four windows. They move from the **PASSIVE zone** of relating to kids into the **ACTIVE zone**. In the next chapter we will consider what a fully engaged KidUnique adult looks like and how personally he or she takes this work. You will be able to assess how you are doing and how you can move into full engagement. The following four chapters give the details of the four-window model and how to unleash its power in the life of a kid. Then, you will be encouraged to do a resentment assessment before extending an invitation for a kid to join the process of discovery. The last part of this book contains a *31-Day Experience* to help kids directly discover who they are.

I can't wait to see what will happen as you step up to the plate and get intentional about this task. I know you will grow as much as the kid you love.

"An adult who is engaged in KidUnique turns loose the power of the four windows."

21

WHAT KIDS NEED MOST

Chapter One

It's Personal!...the power of full engagement

"To raise a healthy child, that child must have at least one adult who is irrationally involved in his or her life."

Dr. Urie Bronfenbrenner
Professor of Human Development - Cornell University

"Our chief want is someone who will inspire us to be what we know we could be."

Ralph Waldo Emerson

Very few times in life have I gotten into a fight or been pushed to the point of wanting to hit someone. When I was 13, I wanted to hit Robby Conrad. Looking back now, I know Robby was just being stupid when he called my younger brother Brian a "retard." But to me it wasn't funny, and the words needed to be taken back. Brian has Down Syndrome. I remember chasing Robby across the yard, into his house, down the hall, and into his room. I grabbed the shirt of this bigger, tougher kid, who could wipe the street with me on a normal day, and shoved him against the wall. I told him to take back the words or I would feed them to him through his bloodied pie-hole. I screamed that if he ever, and I meant ever, made a comment like that again, I'd rip his head off and shove it someplace dark. He backed down, apologizing for his words. In that moment, Brian's honor was restored because I took personally how my brother was treated.

What do you take personally? Successful businesspeople take their performance at work personally. Great marriages are made up of two people who take personally how they treat one another. Top athletes take their roles in athletic contests personally. Recently I heard about a conversation an NFL linebacker had with a running back on the opposing team who had just ripped off a 20-yard run. He said, *"Run that play again, pal. Next time you're dead. Next time it's personal."* First-class schoolteachers take what happens in their classrooms personally. Chefs take personally the taste and appearance of meals they create. When it matters most, it's personal.

As a KidUnique adult, I am challenging you to take this personally, this task of helping a kid discover who he or she is. The more personal you take it, the better chance you'll have of really helping a kid.

KidUnique is a call to build a meaningful, life-giving relationship with a kid. It is one way to combat much of the negativity, frustration, and hopelessness felt by the younger generation. It is a strategy that allows us to turn down the volume on a culture whose goal is to negatively shape our kids' values and identity.

If we are going to take this work *personally,* it means we:

1. **Get ready for war**

2. **Move into the ACTIVE zone ... and**

3. **Beat down the big 'R'**

1. No kidding...this is war

KidUnique is a call to arms. This book is more than a fun, practical guide. It is about fighting for the life and well-being of a kid. We can not sell our kids out with a halfhearted effort. It is time to step up and take this seriously. Dr. Urie Bronfenbrenner, professor of human development at Cornell University, has said, *"To raise a healthy child, that child must have at least one adult who is irrationally involved in his or her life."* You get to be that one crazy adult for a season (whether short or long) in a kid's life.

I know you care about positively affecting a young person or you would not bother reading this book. But just thinking about having an impact is not the same as having one. Just wanting to make a difference in a kid's life is not making one. Just knowing how to have an impact is not getting anything done. Our call is to take action with a strategy that will aggressively breathe life into a kid.

If this is not our mindset, the culture will win every time. We are called to lay down our lives for those we love. You love your kid. Jesus said, *"There is no greater love than to lay down one's life for one's friends" (John 15:13).* Laying down your life is painful, rarely fun or practical. Laying down your life will mean you suffer for your kid. When you love someone, your well-being is tied into their well-being. That means that when they are not doing well, you will not be doing well. There is suffering in this. Get used to it. There is no love without suffering. Laying down your life also means you will have to endure. Insights often come slowly and you will need to be patient. In those

"There is no love without suffering. Laying down your life also means you will have to endure."

Stop and record below the name of someone who ACTIVE-ly related to you when you
were young. Record what they did or said
that expressed interest and care.

Who was it?

What they said to me or did for me:

moments you are laying your life down by hanging in with your kid. You have an important role in the life of your kid, and this book will help you know how to accomplish it.

Jesus had an intense commitment to kids. His passion is seen in Mark 10:13-14 where he reminds his disciples of his desire to bless and love kids. Occasionally he had to shake his disciples so that they thought clearly about this task. *One day some parents brought their children to Jesus so he could touch and bless them. But the disciples scolded the parents for bothering him. When Jesus saw what was happening, he was angry with his disciples. He said to them, "Let the children come to me. Don't stop them! For the Kingdom of God belongs to those who are like these children."*

In those moments Jesus was fully present with kids, and they must have loved it. I am sure they never forgot what it was like to be with someone who so completely loved them. God's heart hasn't changed concerning kids. The disciples were PASSIVE when it came to kids; Jesus was ACTIVE in expressing love and interest.

2. The goal = ACTIVE zone living

If you care about kids, God will pull your heart toward the ACTIVE zone of engagement. The ACTIVE zone is where we are fully unleashed to have a positive impact. In the ACTIVE zone we are fighting for a kid's extraordinary life, and when you live there, you will be *living* an extraordinary life. This is the path to changing the world one life at a time. Kids will hear the words God wants them to hear because you refuse to sit passively on the sidelines. You get up, think, pray, and prepare in a way that says to your kid *you matter to me.* Your actions, words, and presence communicate it.

Look at the difference between the PASSIVE zone and ACTIVE zone in the chart on the next page. Slowly read from top down and left to right, considering each of the four windows. We want our behavior to move from left to right. The hope is to live entirely in the right column. The chart lays out the work of how to help a kid discover who he or she is. How we do that will be discussed in the next four chapters, and lived out during the *31-Day Experience*. For now, let's get familiar with the difference between living in the PASSIVE Zone versus the ACTIVE Zone.

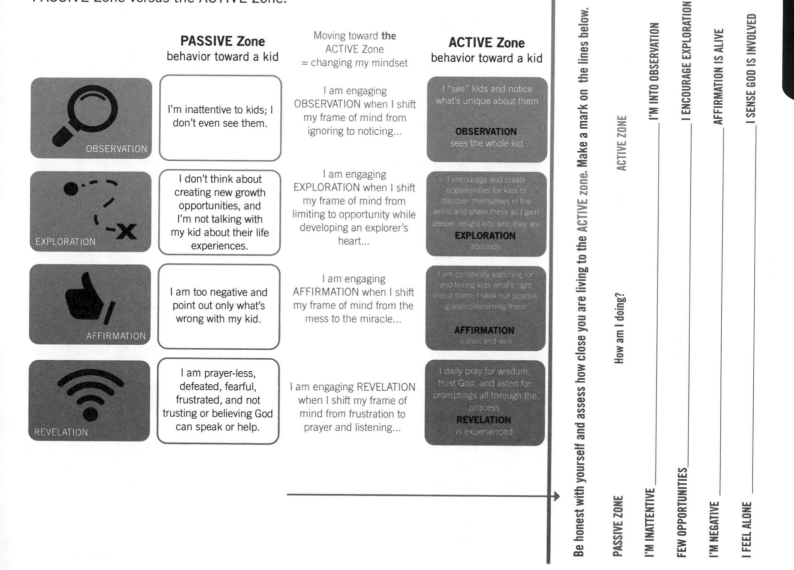

PASSIVE Zone behavior toward a kid	Moving toward the ACTIVE Zone = changing my mindset	**ACTIVE Zone** behavior toward a kid
I'm inattentive to kids; I don't even see them.	I am engaging OBSERVATION when I shift my frame of mind from ignoring to noticing...	I "see" kids and notice what's unique about them **OBSERVATION** sees the whole kid
I don't think about creating new growth opportunities, and I'm not talking with my kid about their life experiences.	I am engaging EXPLORATION when I shift my frame of mind from limiting to opportunity while developing an explorer's heart...	I encourage and create opportunities for kids to discover themselves in the world and share these as I gain deeper insight into who they are **EXPLORATION** abounds
I am too negative and point out only what's wrong with my kid.	I am engaging AFFIRMATION when I shift my frame of mind from the mess to the miracle...	I am constantly watching for and telling kids what's right about them; I seek out positive gossip concerning them **AFFIRMATION** is alive and well
I am prayer-less, defeated, fearful, frustrated, and not trusting or believing God can speak or help.	I am engaging REVELATION when I shift my frame of mind from frustration to prayer and listening...	I daily pray for wisdom, trust God, and listen for promptings all through the process **REVELATION** is experienced

Be honest with yourself and assess how close you are living to the ACTIVE zone. Make a mark on the lines below.

How am I doing?

ACTIVE ZONE

I'M INTO OBSERVATION _____

I ENCOURAGE EXPLORATION _____

AFFIRMATION IS ALIVE _____

I SENSE GOD IS INVOLVED _____

PASSIVE ZONE

I'M INATTENTIVE _____

FEW OPPORTUNITIES _____

I'M NEGATIVE _____

I FEEL ALONE _____

3. Beat down the big 'R'

Resistance[10] is the enemy of anyone who commits to this work. Its presence will be felt each waking moment. Resistance will tell you to do anything but invest in a kid. The big 'R' will say that a kid will be fine without you, that someone else will fill the gap and take up the slack. The big 'R' is a big liar. Get used to the big 'R's taunting and presence. It will suggest that you postpone this task until there is a better time when your schedule is not so full. It will deceive you and say that your kid is fine and doing great.

Resistance is a perpetual nuisance. Do not be surprised when you get exhausted, problems present themselves, and your self-orientation resists the investment you need to make in a kid. Resistance wants us to live in the PASSIVE zone (or keep us there). It will lure us to a neutral attitude and uninvolved stance. Without courage our default condition is the PASSIVE zone—we either fight it or we don't. The choice is ours to make.

You may wonder what to do if life currently has you in the passive zone. Stress, job, and social pressure may have put you there. All it takes to move from left to right is this: *Change your mindset.* Sounds simple. Truth is, it does not come naturally, and it must be an intentional choice.

The ACTIVE zone is both a positive state of mind and a powerful mode of behavior. To get there, we must change our thinking about kids. Make no mistake about it, you can move there right now. In this very moment, you can be moving into the ACTIVE zone.

When we are in the ACTIVE zone we "see" kids and notice what is unique about them. This occurs through the power of ***observation***. When we encourage and create opportunities for kids to discover themselves and then talk about these experiences, ***exploration*** is given a chance and insights are collected. When we constantly tell our kids what is right with them while seeking out other positive perspectives on who they are, ***affirmation*** is in play. When we learn to faithfully pray for the help of God while listening for his voice in the process of discovery, **revelation** will be experienced. This is the behavior and mindset of the ACTIVE zone. If you are there...welcome to the game.

You can do this—believe it

Wanting to live with consistency in the ACTIVE zone says something about you. You long to see your kid grow. Not everyone is like that. In the athletic world, coaches want kids to get *bigger - stronger - faster.* In the academic world, teachers want kids to get *smarter - brighter - deeper.* KidUnique adults long for kids to get *clearer - more secure - more capable - more able to win in life* because at their cores they feel good about who they are. Healthy-hearted adults are thrilled when they see kids thrive and excel. Small-hearted people beat kids down.

When my middle son was in seventh grade he asked me to take him to the gym and teach him how to lift weights, so he could get physically stronger and excel in soccer. The first time we lifted weights together he could barely bench press the 45-pound bar. Five years later, when he was in 11th grade, things had changed. I remember lifting together just after his seventeenth birthday. He put a 45-pound plate on each side of the bench press bar and knocked off 12 reps with the ease of an NFL linebacker. Now it was my turn to lift. I stretched my pecs and said, *"Watch this, little man."* For a reason unknown to me, I was not able to complete my set of 12 repetitions. As I started my lift, I did not have the old zip. Maybe I had low blood sugar or something because at about my sixth repetition I was in trouble. As I was grunting and groaning, struggling to push up my ninth rep, my son began to mock me saying things like, *"Push, you old fart. Come on dad, you are embarrassing me."*

After he assisted me in getting the bar back on the bench, I stood up and called him to come over to me. By the look on his face, I think he thought I was upset. Instead I told him that this was a great day in my life. He laughed and said, *"Yeah, sure. Great day? What are you talking about, dad? Are you celebrating getting old and fat?"* *"Not quite, my young Hercules,"* I responded.

"Son, one of my goals from that day to this has been to help you get stronger than me. Today that is true. This is a great day."

Looking him eye to eye I said, *"Landan, do you remember when we came into this weight room five years ago and you couldn't lift the bar, let alone an additional 90 pounds?"* He nodded. I said, *"Son, one of my goals from that day to this has been to help you get stronger than me. Today that is true. This is a great day. You've grown. I love to see you grow. I can't wait until you are so strong that I have to follow you around the weight room and take plates off the bars just to work out with you."* Today he is in his late 20s, and he is both a physical specimen and a secure young man. He lettered in two college sports, weighs 190 pounds with 6 percent body fat, and as they say...he's ripped. Truth is, if I had a body like his, I'd be a nudist.

What is your mindset and heart condition as you think about your kid? Do you want to see her grow past you? Do you want him to get *bigger - stronger - faster - clearer - more secure - more confident - more mature* in life? I'm guessing you do.

Will you commit to get on their team and learn to bring your best to them in this next season of life? Resistance will challenge you. Your life will get busy and occasionally overwhelming. So what? A kid is looking to you to be someone who shows up and helps. Be that man or woman. Get fully in the game. Memorize the difference between the ACTIVE zone mindset and the PASSIVE zone mindset. Then pray daily for the strength to live there. Now let's turn to the four-window model and start living this out.

"Resistance will challenge you. Your life will get busy and occasionally overwhelming. So what? A kid is looking to you to be someone who shows up and helps."

 # WHERE WE LOOK TO SEE KIDS

Chapter Two
OBSERVATION...the power of seeing kids

"Love begins with the seeing of the other."
Anthony DeMello

"You can observe a lot just by watching."
Ralph Waldo Emerson

Observation: the activity of 'seeing' something or someone

Gillian Lynne is one of the most accomplished choreographers of our time. Along with Andrew Lloyd Webber, she created some of the most successful musical theater productions in history, such as *Cats* and *The Phantom of the Opera*. Gillian would never have experienced the joy of success and living from her "true self" without the help of one man who understood the power of the Observation window.

At age 8, Gillian's future did not look so bright. She was experiencing trouble at school. She was late in turning in her assignments when she did them. Her handwriting was atrocious. She scored poorly on tests and was often a disruption to her entire class. Gillian's teacher believed she had a learning disorder and considered moving her to a school for children with special needs. This happened in the 1930s before the ADHD epidemic swept through the public schools. Today she most likely would have been diagnosed with attention deficit/hyperactivity disorder and prescribed Ritalin®.

The school sent a letter to Gillian's parents describing their concerns. Gillian's mom jumped into action and took her to a psychologist for assessment. Ken Robinson, in his wonderful book, *The Element*, describes what happened next. I have italicized a number of phrases.

> Gillian told me that she remembers being invited into a large oak-paneled room with leather-bound books on the shelves. Standing in the room next to a large desk was an imposing man in a tweed jacket. He took Gillian to the far end of the room and sat her down on a huge leather sofa. Gillian's feet didn't quite touch the floor, and the setting made her wary. Nervous about the impression she would make, she sat on her hands so that she wouldn't fidget.
>
> The psychologist went back to his desk, and for the next twenty minutes, he asked Gillian's mother about the difficulties Gillian was having at school and the problems the school said she was causing. While he didn't direct any of the questions at Gillian, *he watched her carefully the entire time...*

Eventually, Gillian's mother and the psychologist stopped talking. The man rose from his desk, walked to the sofa, and sat next to the little girl.

'Gillian, you've been very patient, and I thank you for that,' he said. 'But I'm afraid you'll have to be patient for a little longer. I need to speak to your mother privately now. We're going to go out of the room for a few minutes. Don't worry; we won't be very long.'

Gillian nodded apprehensively, and the two adults left her sitting there on her own. But as he was leaving the room, the psychologist leaned across his desk and turned on the radio.

As soon as they were in the corridor outside the room, the doctor said to Gillian's mother, 'Just stand here for a moment, and *watch what she does.'* There was a window into the room, and they stood to one side of it, where Gillian couldn't see them. Nearly immediately, Gillian was on her feet, moving around the room to the music. *The two adults stood watching quietly for a few minutes,* transfixed by the girl's grace. Anyone would have noticed there was something natural—even primal—about Gillian's movements. Just as they would have surely caught the expression of utter pleasure on her face.

At last, the psychologist turned to Gillian's mother and said, 'You know, Mrs. Lynne, Gillian isn't sick. She's a dancer. Take her to a dance school.'

Little Gillian, the girl with the high-risk future, became...someone who has brought pleasure to millions and earned millions of dollars. This happened *because someone looked deep into her eyes—someone who had seen children like her before and knew how to read the signs.* Someone else might have put her on medication and told her to calm down. But Gillian wasn't a problem child. She didn't need to go away to a special school.

*She just needed to be who she really was.*11

"She didn't need to go away to a special school. She just needed to be who she really was."

Those who leverage the Observation window understand that there is a story unfolding right before their eyes in the lives of the kids they love and they slow down enough to "see" it. They recognize that kids behave the way they do for a reason. Often behavior is motivated by such surface things as anger or frustration or illness. None of those motivated Gillian's behavior. There was something deeper happening in that 8-year-old little girl. It took love and discernment to see it.

Gillian's behavior was driven by her nature—something in her DNA. Gillian is a great example of KidUnique. She had a gift that may never have been given to the world had it not been for one man who *"watched her carefully the entire time."* Fortunately, she had a mother who responded to his insights accordingly. That is the heart of the Observation window—watching our kids carefully and noticing their uniqueness.

Observation is the first window we peer through as we attempt to help kids discover who they are. It is a powerful force in the discovery process. It is the work of attentively watching the one we care for. It is studying a kid as he or she grows up and recording glimpses of what we see at any given moment along the way. Observation communicates both interest and concern. Anthony DeMello is right: Love does begin with the "*seeing*" of the other.

There is a verse of scripture from the Old Testament that says, **For the Lord sees clearly what a man does, examining every path he takes (Proverbs 5:21).** Inherent in God's loving nature is that he "sees" his creation. God pays attention to those he loves. **Like God**[12], we will pay attention to the kid we love. In doing so we communicate to them that they have value and are worth our attention and time.

THE PROBLEM OF DISTRACTIONS

There are many distractions that can turn our vision away from the Observation window and keep us from being able to actively see our kids. Adults who reside in the ACTIVE zone of Observation eliminate these so they can keep watching their kid. Let us consider three such distractions.

#1: DRIBBLING WITH YOUR HEAD DOWN

It is important not to do what I did as I was learning to dribble a basketball in high school. For me to possess the basketball for any length of time, I had to constantly look down to be sure I would not lose control. This crippled my ability to see my teammates and opportunities to score. Breaking this habit was challenging. It took practice and the help of a coach. Whenever the coach would notice me looking down at the ball he would yell, *"Webster, get your head up so you can see the open man down the court."* I understood that if I wanted to become a good basketball player (and one day make the varsity team) I would have to break the habit of dribbling with my head down. I did, but it wasn't easy.

The same is true for KidUnique adults. It is very easy to live with our heads down, preoccupied with our own little worlds. A close friend told me that when he got home from a business trip one Friday, he zipped home from the airport and picked up his son so they could have dinner and get caught up. As they were looking at the menu, my friend got a few business text messages. In the middle of quickly shooting back a response, he got another text message. This one was from his son sitting across the table. The message said, *"Hey dad, how about putting down the phone?"* That is dribbling with your head down.

All of us get preoccupied. Our challenge is to learn how to manage our lives so that we can see kids "up the court." At the core of KidUnique is the ability to multi-task. Task one is to manage our own lives well so that we can see others. Task two is to focus on (and really see) others. We need to focus our multitasking skills to include our kids and others as a top priority. It is impossible to see kids if we have our heads buried in our own problems. Living with our heads down, whether self-absorbed, filled with anxiety, or mad about something, blinds us from seeing opportunities to encourage and take part in a kid's life on a meaningful level. All of these push our vision downward, minimizing our sight. The better we manage our lives, the easier it will be to see our kids.

Is there something in your personal world currently causing you to dribble with your head down?

What is it?

#2: THE MESS CLOUDS THE MIRACLE

When you engage a kid, it will not take long for you to notice something. They are both a miracle and a mess. Every kid has an upside and a downside. Welcome to planet earth. John Ortberg has written a book titled *Everybody's Normal Till You Get To Know Them*. That title is so true. Chances are when you meet new people you are impressed—at least at first you are. They attempt to be charming, polite, and interesting. They present themselves well. But given enough time you would find something about them that bugs you, and I am guessing it would not take too long.

The fact that every kid has both an upside and a downside can be distracting. The tendency is to get stuck at the downside. Some people seem to live to point out only the downside of others. If that is you, ask God to change your heart before spending time with kids, because you will do more harm than good. The Scripture tells us *a wise person stays calm when insulted (Proverbs 12:16)* and *love covers a multitude of sins (1 Peter 4:8).* Kids are works in progress, and our love must be big enough and mature enough to look beyond the stuff that bugs us and see what is brilliant in a kid.

The simple truth is that Observation reveals both. Some of their characteristics will delight your heart, and others will put your head in a vice. The temptation that we must resist is to solely focus on the "mess" side of things. It is relatively easy to see who a kid is *not*. It takes love, time, and discernment to see who a kid *is*.

Which part of a kid's identity do you think gets the most attention? On average, do teachers, friends, and parents remind kids of the mess part or the miracle part? There are profound differences in adults who were treated well as kids and continually reminded that they were miracles. KidUnique is all about increasing a kid's appreciation for the miracle side of who he or she is. It is about noticing what's right and generously communicating it. It's cheering on the upside and loving in the middle of the downside. If this is hard for you, ask God to help you both see and call out the miracle aspect of your kid.

Is there something messy in my kid's life that prevents me from seeing the miracle of who he or she is on a deeper level?

What is it?

A couple of Christmases ago I gave each of my grown sons a framed letter. These letters were personally composed and identified seven or eight specific positive characteristics I saw in each of them. I called the gift the *"What's Right With You"* letters. I spent hours focusing on each of my sons so that I could name what was unique about each. I do not think these letters were what they wanted for Christmas but I understand today that they were what they needed. I just returned from visiting my middle son in Texas. He is 27 years old at the time of this writing. While in his apartment I noticed that he still has his letter on his nightstand. He has given me permission to share it.

Landan –

Without question, fathering you has been one of the best experiences of my life. I have loved being (and still love being) your dad. I know that there have been times when I've been a good and wise father. And, I know that at other times I've angered you, frustrated you, been stupid, and generally made a mess of things as a dad. Thank God for forgiveness and do-overs.

Anyway…this Christmas I sat down and spent some time reflecting on what's RIGHT with you and what I love about you. We each live in our own skin and know where we screw up and fall short. Who needs to be reminded of that, right? As I thought about this, I realized that I haven't told you in a while what's RIGHT with you.

So, here goes…my reminder of what's RIGHT with you.

First, you have *a genius way of seeing life*. Some may have a higher IQ, but few have the brilliance you possess. Your ability to see into things and solve complex issues is something you will celebrate as you age and get more experience. Trust me Landan, you have this gift! You are creatively bright and insightful.

Second, you are *hard working*. Nothing has come easy for you and you've discovered that hard work gets you to where you want to be. You've demonstrated this in transforming yourself from a chubby Jr. High kid into a model of fitness. You've shown this as you have learned strategies to compensate for learning challenges. You were a scholar athlete in high school and get A's and B's in college. This is truly amazing! And, you've shown this as you've prepared yourself for soccer and swimming. Even though you didn't make the soccer team this last year, it wasn't because you weren't prepared.

Third, you are *brave and have the ability to bounce back.* You have encountered more disappointments in life than most people. Some with sports, some with women, some with studies, some with unfulfilled dreams. Through each of these you didn't run away. Rather, you decided to look them in the face, grow through them, and get up and move on. Courage is a wonderful thing and I see it in you everyday! This inspires me and I find strength in your courage.

Fourth, you are *a deep and loyal friend.* Those who know you best understand this about you. The down side of this is that most of your friends aren't as loyal as you and that hurts. But, being a close and trusted friend will make you a great husband and dad. And another thought on this...I pity the fool who wounds a friend of yours because they have just invited a boat-load of trouble from you. Oh yeah, you are a good friend. (By the way...thanks for being my friend!)

Fifth, you can *dance.* Dang, the boy can get a move on. Boogie woogie is your middle name and booty shaking is your game. I have no idea where this ability came from. But, shoot, the boy can dance.

Sixth, you *refuse to settle.* Most people set puny goals and low standards. You don't! You set high standards when it comes to fitness, friendships, and females. You also refuse to be inauthentic in your walk with God. This is a high standard. You know that if it isn't real, it's not worth it. A man gets in this life what he goes after and you are going after the right things. Keep your standards high, Landan.

> *"The fact that every kid has both an upside and a downside can be distracting. The tendency is to get stuck at the downside."*

OBSERVATION

And seventh, you *love excellence*. You have a sense of what should be and can be. You want an excellent life, an excellent career, an excellent body, an excellent family, and an excellent faith. Keep reaching son and you will get what your heart longs for. Do you remember when a couple of your high school friends were your standard of excellence? These guys are not an issue anymore. The sky is the limit for you. Never doubt that!

Not bad...seven RIGHT things about you: *a genius way of seeing life, hard working, brave, deep and loyal friend, dancer, refuses to settle, and loves excellence.*

I celebrate these about you Landan...you should too. Know I love and believe in you son.

As always...for you...anything, anytime, anywhere.

Dad

The act of creating this letter was meaningful. Something profound and visceral happened in me as I wrote it. Doing this task made me focus on the miracle side—the what's-right-with-you side—the upside—of each guy. At the end of the *31-Day Experience* you will be given the opportunity to write such a letter for your kid.

#3: THE PREDICTABLE IRRITATIONS OF DAILY LIFE

Years ago, when my sons were young and not spread out all over the country, I awakened to something that had the potential to crush my love for them. It became apparent to me that if I did not come to grips with this issue and develop a strategy to overcome it, I would not be able to "see" or love my boys the way they needed.

The issue had to do with the predictable irritations of daily life. You know what these are—messy rooms, bickering, fighting (brothers do that you know—sisters, too), dirty cars, rudeness, laziness, insensitivity, general

"Doing this task made me focus on the miracle side—the what's-right-with-you side—the upside—of each guy."

irresponsibility, and a hundred other irritations that are part of life and growing up.

Here is an example. One evening after work I walked into the house and noticed a literal clothing explosion had occurred. Shirts, shoes, socks, and schoolbooks were everywhere. Believe it or not, this would bug the heck out of me. Intercepting my first response, which was anger, was critical. If I didn't intercept my reaction, the family would witness an eruption of *Mount Big Daddy Webster.* On other evenings I would walk into a fight the guys were having over some petty issue. The fact is that these predictable annoyances threatened my relationships with my sons. Annoyances can put the relationship you have with your kid in jeopardy, too. They easily sidetrack us and pull us down.

As you engage a kid, you will be met with predictable irritations. Get used to it. Sometimes kids will do things that annoy you on purpose. They may be late for meetings. They might have habits that bug you. They may just have an "attitude" that sets you off. I came up with a strategy to deal with this challenge, inspired by a close friend. It involved *prayer* and my *priority list.*

On the drive home each night from work I would mentally leave the concerns of the job at the office. A close friend called his ride home from work each day *"the nine-mile drive."* That is how far it was from his office to his house. During the drive home he told me he would pray and entrust the stresses, pressures, and worries of the office to God. Then he would attempt to reset his mind and heart so that he could engage his kids. He told himself that no matter what the house looked like or what was going on, the first thing he would do when he walked in was to hug his wife and kids. No matter what, that came first! Maybe you will need to pray on the drive to Starbucks® where you are meeting your kid. Or maybe it will be on the walk up the stairs to your kid's room. These brief prayers opened me to God's help. Visualizing the potential irritations in the house enabled me to choose to live above them.

What is the predictable irritation you will face today that holds the power to distract you from seeing the miracle aspect of your kid?

"As you engage a kid, you will be met with predictable irritations. Get used to it."

I would pray that God would grace me with the capacity to fly above the little stuff so that I could communicate the important stuff. I asked God to help me look right past the mess and move toward my sons, reminding them that I love them even when things are messy. I discovered over time that the strength of my relationship with each boy motivated him to grow up and become more responsible. I learned that if they questioned my love at their core, things only got worse. So, right toward the top of my *priority list* was convincing them by my behavior and words that, no matter what is currently going on, good or bad, messy or neat, easy or hard, they are loved by me. That mattered most.

You can sail above the predictable irritations of daily life, too. Before you connect with your kid, pray for the maturity and buoyancy to float above. Never let little things get in the way of the most important things.

Looking through the Observation Window

Pause for a moment and reread what it means to be in the ACTIVE zone as it applies to the Observation window.

PASSIVE Zone behavior toward a kid	Moving toward the ACTIVE Zone = changing my mindset	**ACTIVE Zone** behavior toward a kid

I'm inattentive to kids; I don't even see them.	I am engaging OBSERVATION when I shift my frame of mind from ignoring to noticing...	I "see" kids and notice what's unique about them **OBSERVATION** sees the whole kid

We want to move from inattention to "seeing" kids, which will involve noticing what is unique about them. We want to observe the whole kid. That is a left to right movement. To get this task done we need to answer three questions.

- *HOW DO I OBSERVE MY KID?*
- *WHAT DO I LOOK FOR?*
- *HOW DO I ENGAGE MY KID WITH WHAT I SEE?*

* _____ (name of your kid)

is _____

_____
(what is true and unique)

* _____ (name of your kid)

is _____

_____
(what is true and unique)

* _____ (name of your kid)

is _____

_____
(what is true and unique)

* _____ (name of your kid)

is _____

_____
(what is true and unique)

HOW DO I OBSERVE MY KID?—LIKE A SLEUTH!

Observation is as simple as just paying attention. As Yogi Berra said, *"You can observe a lot just by watching."* Look away from yourself and other distractions and look at your kid. Watch when they play, study and interact with people and life. Notice reactions. What do you see?

Rick Lawrence, a friend and the editor of GROUP Magazine, recently suggested to me that to observe a kid well we must become a sleuth. He is right. We should strive to become like the famous detective Sherlock Holmes with his amazing skills of observation. He would notice a small amount of yellow sand on the shoe of a suspect and know that that sand came from the beach at Bimba Bimba Island. That observation would break the case. His powers of perception were astounding. Great detectives pay attention to details, and sense and see things that others do not. They look for clues that others miss. Gillian's psychologist did this.

Observation is about the slow process of solving the mystery of who your kid is. It will not happen overnight. It will take many times of both seeing and interacting. Grow to understand that observing is as simple as watching, listening, and noticing.

WHAT DO I LOOK FOR?—THE 'PULL' AND 'DRAW' FACTOR

Identify first what is obvious about your kid. Given the history you have together, what have you noticed is true? Just think off the top of your head. Maybe these questions will help trigger some thoughts.

- *What are some likes and dislikes?*

- *What are some interests?*

- *What is unique about your kid?*

- *What is he or she naturally good at?*

- *Do you support these?*

- *Do you express interest?*

I am guessing that was not too tough of an exercise for you. Over the years I have asked parents to describe what their kids are like and most can go on and on. These are the kind of responses I have heard...

"Bobby is serious; you can see it on his face."

"Jill is competitive; she shows this by always wanting to win."

"Logan is curious; he has his nose in a book every day."

"Harper is lighthearted; she doesn't seem to have a care in the world."

"Lucy is intense; she gets right in your face about what interests her."

"Bryan is organized; he can not stand it when his stuff gets cluttered."

"Jose loves being challenged; he hates being bored."

"Keesha is musical; she wants music playing all the time."

"John takes stuff apart; he wants to know how things work."

"Rory loves music; he says he hears music in colors."

"Nancy loves to entertain; she puts on a show when friends are here."

"Lance is sensitive; he can sense when someone is hurting."

These insights came to adults as they looked through the Observation window. Some are more profound than others, but each is true.

If you can, list what your kid loves—what is pulling at and drawing him or her.

* Name:

What is drawing my kid:

* Name:

What is drawing my kid:

* Name:

What is drawing my kid:

* Name:

What is drawing my kid:

Let us think now on a deeper level about your kid. As I have already mentioned, kids behave the way they do for a reason. There are innate passions and interests living in your kid that will affect behavior and what he or she is drawn to. We must train ourselves to watch for what *pulls* at our kids. Read that last sentence again.

The things kids truly love "call" to them. Music, movement, and dance called to Gillian. What draws a kid is like a whisper in his or her head that we cannot hear. Deep interests pull at our kids. If they love art, the canvas calls. If they love music, the instrument calls. It they love math, numbers call. If they love dance, movement calls. If they love basketball, the gym calls. What is calling to your kid?

There is a difference between things that kids are pushed into versus what they are drawn toward. We can push our kids into things that we think are cool but are a thousand miles from who they are. The "pull factor" in a kid's life is far more important than the push factor. We want to discover what pulls them and encourage investigation. We want to figure out what is unique about them **on the upside**13. This does not happen often enough. I know it did not happen for one of my close friends.

From an early age a friend of mine was "drawn" to aviation. He loved everything about flying and knew being a pilot would perfectly fit him. As a child he would build model airplanes, fly them until they crashed, and rebuild them again. When young he would ride his bike to the local airport and hour after hour watch planes take off and land. Today he is not a pilot. Why? Because his dad did not think it was a good idea. His dad killed his dream when he was 17. When my friend approached his dad to tell him he wanted to apply to the Air Force Academy and eventually become a pilot, his father simply told him it wasn't going to happen and to think about another option. My friend should have been true to himself and chased after what he loved in spite of his dad, but the voice of a father is a powerful thing in the life of a young man. May we never do such a thing to the kids we love.

"When my friend approached his dad to tell him he wanted to apply to the Air Force Academy and eventually become a pilot, his father simply told him it wasn't going to happen and to think about another option...may we never do such a think to the kids we love."

List someone who somewhere along the way helped you see the good in you.

Who was it?

What did they see in you?

Why was it important?

HOW DO I ENGAGE MY KID WITH WHAT I OBSERVE?— PASS ON THE "GLIMMERS"

KidUnique is about relationship. It is hard to know what our kids are feeling or thinking all the time. The fun part of this relationship is building up kids by flowing truthful, positive, uplifting, life-giving information to them. It is a kick to get kids thinking about how God has made them and what that might mean to their futures. Many kids constantly struggle with feeling overwhelmed by the challenges of life. We get to breathe life into them as we share our observations.

I have mentioned that most of us are quicker to see the downside of a kid than the upside. You may be able to identify in a moment three things that bug you to death, but it may really take some work to identify the upside. Before you interact with your kid, take the list of stuff that bugs you and commit it to God. Remember that you did not get to be the wonderful, secure, contributing adult you are without a lot of grace. Someone somewhere along the way helped you see the good in you.

The action you can take when you gain an insight is to simply tell your kid what you see and then engage in conversation about it. Be intentional about doing this. When you drive to the store, take a kid with you to share something you have noticed. Go on individual walks to just talk. Or, if a kid is open to it, have a nightly recap of what you saw in him or her. If you have a number of kids, share with one per night. Maybe you did not have a big insight that day, but you can remind them of your love for them.

If we were to take the parental responses I listed earlier, here is how they might each follow up and share with their kid.

"Bobby my boy, I love that you take things seriously. Do you see that you take things seriously? Let me tell you why that's important. Many people don't care about anything..."

"Hey Jill, it's cool that you are competitive. That intensity will help you as you grow up. Do you see that in yourself?"

"Logan, I'm amazed at your curiosity and interest in learning. Do you see that in yourself? Let me tell you why that's important. Too many people stop learning and growing..."

"Harper, your lighthearted spirit lifts everyone around you. That's wonderful. Do you see that in yourself? Let me tell you why that's important. Many people live under the burden of life and need people to remind them life is a gift..."

"Lucy, I enjoy how you dig into life with intensity. That's special about you. Do you see that in yourself? Let me tell you why that's important. Many people are apathetic and just let life pass them by..."

"Bryan, it's amazing how organized you are. That is so cool. Do you see that in yourself? Let me tell you why that's important. People who accomplish significant things in life are often the most organized..."

"Jose, I'm blown away at your willingness to take on challenges. Do you see that in yourself? Let me tell you why that's important. The world needs people who are unafraid to tackle problems..."

"Keesha, it is so wonderful that you live with a song in your heart. Do you see that in yourself? Let me tell you why that's important. Music has the power to lift and change people..."

You get the idea. You will know there has been a sighting of something unique when you get a glimmer of something about your kid. I love what the Scripture says about Mary, Jesus' mother. She experienced sightings as she cared for the Lord. These sightings gave her glimmers into who Jesus was. Watch for the glimmers as you observe your kid. You will sense and see them. Twice in the Gospel of Luke the Scripture says, ***Mary treasured all these things, pondering*** *them in her heart (Luke 2:19 NASB).* She recognized the unique identity of Jesus. You must identify the unique identity of the kid you love.

When you talk with your kid you will not have the whole picture, but you will have a small piece of the puzzle. Your relationship will be characterized by many of these brief "glimmer" conversations. Keep your eyes open and watch. Celebrate who your kid is in each conversation.

Just imagine, when you see something cool about your kid, you are seeing something God has known since the day he or she was conceived. King David was ambushed one day by the wonder of his identity. In a moment of clarity he prayed, *I will give thanks to You, for I am fearfully and wonderfully made; wonderful are Your works, and my soul knows it very well (Psalm 139:14 NASB).* Won't it be great when our kids have that understanding? We want our kids to know how wonderful they are on a *"soul"* level.

> "Just imagine, when you see something cool about your kid, you are seeing something God has known since the day he or she was conceived."

We want kids to walk away from our times together pondering the fact that they are wonderful and gifted and unique. This is God's heart toward them. You get to deliver the news over and over again as you gain insight concerning who they are. The song you sing to them will have a consistent melody, but the words of the verses change as you see more and more of what is true about your kid. Is that a great gift to give? Is that a work that is worth doing? Will a hundred of these brief conversations over the next year change how your kid sees himself or herself? You know the answer.

In the *31-Day Experience* at the end of this book, you will be given additional ideas and applications that will help you with the Observation window. For now maybe it would be good to find and engage your kid with just one or two of the things you love about him or her. Get active and have fun.

ACTION Plan for the Observation Window

	PASSIVE Zone adults are...	Moving toward the ACTIVE Zone I will be...	ACTIVE Zone adults are...

OBSERVATION

I'm inattentive to kids.

Key defining word:
Ignoring

1. Dribbling with my head up
2. Seeing the miracle, not just the mess
3. Anticipating predictable irritations

To observe well I must:
- Become a sleuth
- Identify the "pull" factor
- Share freely the "glimmers"

Seeing kids, noticing what's unique about them and telling them.
When we do this we are "Seeing" and observation is in play.

Place a mark on the line above that identifies how close you are to the ACTIVE Zone.

What action will you take today to move more toward the ACTIVE Zone? Be specific.

What adult friend is praying for you as you participate in KidUnique? Call that person and say "thanks."

WHERE WE LOOK TO SEE KIDS

Chapter Three

EXPLORATION...the power of inspiring kids to discover and learn about themselves

"Do not follow where there is a path, go instead where there is no path and leave a trail."

Ralph Waldo Emerson

"Twenty years from now you will be more disappointed by the things you didn't do than by the ones you did do. So throw off the bowlines. Sail away from the safe harbor. Catch the trade winds in your sails. Explore. Dream. Discover."

Mark Twain

Exploration: the activity of searching thoroughly to find something or someone

My youngest son recently graduated from Michigan State University. During his senior year my wife and I drove out to watch one of his soccer games. Afterward Logan talked us into taking him, his girlfriend Amanda, Molly, Fil, Brad, and Katie to dinner. The joys of having a kid in college! The hostess at Mongolian BBQ sat us in a small side room with a round table, making conversation easy. I love every one of Logan's friends. They are bright, fun-loving, high-potential kids. During lunch Amanda's roommate, Katie, went off on a rant about how she was a senior and had spent all her money on college and she still didn't know what she wanted to do with her life. We all listened respectfully. When she was done there was a silence around the table.

I looked across the table at her and asked, *"Katie, do you want some help with that?"* She said, *"Help with what?"* I responded, *"Help with knowing what you should do with your life."* She gave me a puzzled look that expressed...you mean there is help with this issue? I leaned over to Logan and asked for permission to share a thought that might be helpful to all these graduating seniors. He said, *"Go for it dad, just don't embarrass me."* I smiled and said to her...

Katie, if you are going to understand what you should do with your life you have to increase your level of self-awareness. To do this you need to pay attention to when you come alive inside. A question I regularly ask people I coach is, *'Where's the life for you?'*

This is important to be able to answer because investing your life in something that only drains you, is not interesting to you, or does not give you life, will be a slow death. Way too many people show up at work every day and attempt to give to the world what they do not have. The result is depression and minimal contribution. What you do have to give the world, your gifts and talents, will be revealed partly by what awakens you inside. That's what I mean when I ask, *'Where's the life?'* Or, maybe better stated, *'When have you and do you come alive inside?'*

"I looked across the table at her and asked, 'Katie, do you want some help with that?' She said, 'Help with what?' "

Think back over your years here at MSU and even earlier than that. What classes were you drawn to? Which ones weren't work to attend? Think about all the various jobs and service opportunities you have had. Which ones resulted in filling you with life rather than draining life from you? What were you doing when you felt alive inside? Take an hour and write down your thoughts and then kick them around with people who know you best and love you. I think you will be fascinated by what you learn about yourself. As you do this, there will be clues that can help you solve the mystery of you.

Think about it this way...imagine if we could move this dining room table out of this room and replace it with a baby grand piano. There are 88 keys with corresponding strings in a standard baby grand. Now, imagine that we remove the top of the piano exposing all the strings. Do you know what will happen if I lean into the opening of the piano and shout loudly the word *"hey?"* I just make a short abrupt scream of the one syllable word, *hey.* Any idea what will happen?" (She shook her head.) The string that was tuned closest to the resonate frequency of the note I shouted would vibrate. It cannot *not* vibrate. It will resonate with the note I broadcast from my mouth.

That's what happens in you as you get around things that give you life. Something vibrates inside you. Pay attention to when the strings that God has planted in your soul vibrate. Why is it that Logan comes alive when we talk about business and multiplying money? Why does Amanda come alive when we talk about medicine and healing the sick? Why does Fil come alive when we talk about design and architecture? Why does Molly come alive when we talk about kids and teaching school? Why does Brad come alive when it's dinner time? It's a strange thing, huh?

Here's what I'm trying to say—topics, social needs, challenges, and issues all broadcast certain frequencies. The strings in you will vibrate when you are around your core interests. Pay attention to when they vibrate. You will know they are vibrating when there is interest. You will know they are vibrating when there is energy rising up within you. You will know when they are vibrating because you will want to talk about them and engage them on deeper levels. It is a mystery to me why specific strings are in you and not in someone else. I just know they are there and as real as your blonde hair. When you wake up to this you are on your way to knowing what you should do with your life.

"What were you doing when you felt alive inside?"

The Exploration window is about a kid exploring life and discovering himself or herself along the way. In my conversation with Katie, I was inviting her to seriously explore her reactions to past life experiences. I wanted to see her search more thoroughly to find the deeper truths of who she is. Katie went to school every day. She sat in classes. She related to people and had a part-time job. She had hobbies. She had a history of life experience. What she was not attentive to was her reactions to her experiences and what they might mean. If I were to fully engage her in the KidUnique process, I would spend far more time mining into her life experiences to surface insights and messages about her identity. When we are looking through the Exploration window, we are learning to use opportunities to discover insights about our kids.

Pause for a moment. Before we move ahead, reread what it means to be in the ACTIVE zone as it applies to the Exploration window. Don't forget that the goal is to always be moving from left to right in our thinking and behavior.

PASSIVE Zone behavior toward a kid		Moving toward the ACTIVE Zone = changing my mindset	ACTIVE Zone behavior toward a kid
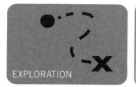	I don't think about creating new growth opportunities and I'm not talking with my kid(s) about their life experiences.	I am engaging EXPLORATION when I shift my frame of mind from limiting to opportunity while developing an explorer's heart...	I encourage and create opportunities for kids to discover themselves in the world and share these as I gain deeper insight into who they are. **EXPLORATION** abounds

Developing An Explorer's Heart

KidUnique adults learn how to look through the Exploration window by developing an explorer's heart. Explorers are restless to discover. Explorers encourage new adventures and love to see kids take new opportunities. Adults with an explorer's heart push into new ground, understanding on ever-deeper levels the terrain of a kid's life. As they do this they inspire their kids to value the exploration process. There are four specific characteristics of an explorer's heart important to consider. As we embody each of these we will be looking through the Exploration window. Let's consider each of them.

AN EXPLORER'S HEART #1—INSPIRES KIDS TO ENGAGE LIFE OPPORTUNITIES AND ADVENTURES

Most adults delight in creating opportunities for kids to grow and explore. Some of us can provide more than others but everything in a kid's daily schedule is an opportunity to learn and discover. School, classes, sports, clubs, hobbies, field trips, books, mission trips, church activities, movies, music, friends...all these evoke a reaction inside a kid. Close your eyes for a moment and run through your mind all the activities your kids have been a part of this last week. How aware are you of their reactions to these experiences?

AN EXPLORER'S HEART #2—PAYS CLOSE ATTENTION TO REACTIONS AND COLLECTS INSIGHTS

The Apostle Paul wanted the kid he loved to take personal exploration seriously. He instructed young Timothy to *pay close attention to yourself (1 Timothy 4:16 NASB)*. When the Apostle Paul said that, he wasn't telling Timothy to be selfish or self-absorbed. He was simply reminding Timothy that the example of his life was critical to his ministry success.

I think he was also reminding Timothy that paying close attention to yourself could be useful—it will tell you things about yourself. Paul wanted young Timothy to be aware of the *nonstop source of data, information, and insight that was right in front of him* in the form of his reactions to life. How Timothy interacted with people and responded to challenges revealed truth about him. What was interesting (or uninteresting) to him gave clues into the person of Timothy. The insight generated from reflection could be useful to understanding Timothy's identity.

The same is true for us. As the kids we love bump into life, we pay attention. As they do new things and discover they are good at some and not so good

> *"Adults with an explorer's heart push into new ground, understanding on ever-deeper levels the terrain of a kid's life."*

at others, we pay attention. As opportunities present themselves and our kids are drawn to them or repulsed by them, we pay attention. In our conversations we also encourage our kids to pay attention to their reactions. In the previous chapter we mentioned the "pull" or "draw" factor. Pay attention to that.

This last week your kid probably went to school and sat through classes, worked at a part-time job, did chores, hung out with friends, went to church, read, engaged in hobbies, saw a movie, and participated in activities like sports or clubs. Maybe he or she even tried something new. Were you paying attention? Think back for a moment about his or her week.

PAYING-ATTENTION EXERCISE

Think about the past week in your kid's life. List experiences or opportunities he or she had. What was the reaction? Don't over-evaluate these. Just write what you noticed on the surface. Don't fill in the third column yet.

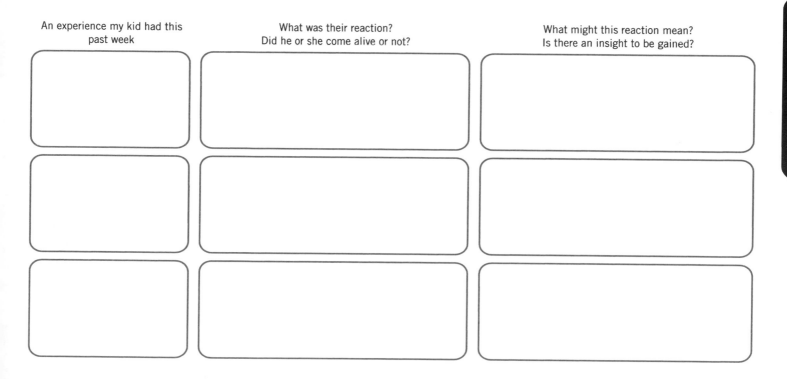

An experience my kid had this past week	What was their reaction? Did he or she come alive or not?	What might this reaction mean? Is there an insight to be gained?

How did you do? Let us take this one step further. Once we encourage exploration and are paying attention to reactions, now we ponder what these reactions mean. Just as I told Katie, pay special attention to when your kid comes alive. Depending upon your kid's age you may suggest carrying a 3x5 card throughout the week to track the moments when he or she felt fully awake and engaged in life. Then kick around these reactions and watch for patterns. Now go back to the previous page and fill in the third column, considering what insight might be gained.

When Logan, my youngest son, was in seventh grade he played soccer for his school team. He was a midfielder until the day the team's goalkeeper was injured. During warm-ups Logan mentioned that the keeper was hurt. I encouraged him to fill in. After a couple minutes of thought he went to the coach and volunteered to be goalkeeper for that game. They were playing their arch rival and it was a big game, as big as a seventh-grade middle school soccer game can be. As I sat on the sidelines I watched something amazing happen. Logan instinctively read the game from the keeper position. He somehow knew when to attack the ball and when to lay back and allow the play to come to him. I was amazed. He was only in seventh grade and had not had any coaching in this position. He was completely relaxed and in control.

In the last minute of the game there was a foul committed by one of his defenders that resulted in a penalty kick. His team held a 1-0 lead at the time. The best player on the opposing team stepped up to take the kick and Logan blocked his shot, preserving the win for his team. In that moment there was life bubbling out of him. He did this little hip-hop boogie-woogie dance move that cracked me up. It was no surprise he was excited...he had just ensured a victory.

My explorer's heart was wondering what was happening on a deeper level inside him. What had allowed him to do so well and be so calm? What did he think of this new experience? How was he reacting inside, and did he even know?

On the drive home after I congratulated him on his victory, I casually asked him if he had fun today? *"Duh?!...Yeahhhhhhh! What do you think?"* was his response. Nothing the matter with a little sarcasm. He's always been a bit cocky and he was in seventh grade, for goodness' sake. I asked if he was nervous at all during the game. *"Not really, Dad. I felt great."* I queried how he knew when to attack the play and when to lay back. He responded, *"I'm not sure. I just did what I thought was the right thing at the time."* When I asked how he knew where the penalty kick was going he said, *"I watched Tyler approach the ball and guessed right. Pretty cool, huh?"* Huh. My last question was, *"Logan, did you have fun...I mean did you feel alive when you were in goal today?"* He said, *"I had a lot of fun Dad, it was a blast."* That was good enough for me. I suggested that he might have a gift and he ought to volunteer to play in goal again to confirm it.

He did, and to make a long story short...he never went back to play in the field again. He could have. He is a good field player. But he became a great goalkeeper. He had a gift. The international talent scout of a European soccer club identified Logan's ability at age 15 and invited him to train three weeks overseas. He rode his gift all the way through college. It all began with him experiencing a new opportunity, identifying the "life" factor, and then engaging him in a conversation about it.

My friend spent last Saturday with his kids playing at the park. He found himself chasing his 3-year-old up a hill covered with rocks. It was kind of dangerous for her, but she was up to the challenge. He said she was fully alive in the adventure of it all. His last comment was that all he could think about was the Exploration window. That is a dad who is paying attention.

As we develop an explorer's heart we will pay attention to opportunities our kids have had both past and present. We will attempt to determine which they have been authentically pulled toward. Then we draw careful conclusions allowing time and more experience to confirm them. Don't forget that artistic kids are drawn to the canvas, stage, choir, or an instrument. Athletic kids are drawn to the gym, track, weight room, or field. Academic kids are drawn to topics, ideas, and books. An explorer's heart celebrates a kid's interests.

> *"My last question was, 'Logan, did you have fun...I mean did you feel alive when you were in goal today?' He said, 'I had a lot of fun Dad, it was a blast.' "*

"...artistic kids are drawn to the canvas, stage, choir, or an instrument. Athletic kids are drawn to the gym, track, weight room, or field. Academic kids are drawn to topics, ideas, and books. An explorer's heart celebrates a kid's interests."

AN EXPLORER'S HEART #3—DOESN'T GET PUSHY OR ONLY EXPLORE THE GROUND THAT'S OFFERED

The dance of engaging a kid in the discovery process can be tricky. Sometimes he or she will want to talk about these things and sometimes not. Learn to read your kid. Encourage and create as many opportunities to explore as possible. Know that some kids will be opportunity junkies. Others, not so much. Be careful not to push him or her into things that meet resistance. Suggest and create opportunities, but let your kid be drawn into what interests him or her. Celebrate your kid's unique interests, not yours. Once he or she participates, ask about the experience. Watch for resonances.

My oldest son, Luke, was drawn into serving behind the scenes when he was young. At 10 years of age he was volunteering doing lighting for the Sunday school program at church. I did not push him into it; he was pulled by something inside him toward it. He loved it. In high school he was part of the drama department. He did not act; he designed lighting for the state champion drama team. From an early age, he has had an eye for design and the aesthetics of environments. Along with this he has always loved music and people. At age 4 I took him to orchestra concerts. He really enjoyed them, often more than I did. His love for music lives on today. Create experiences, watch for reactions, talk about it, and learn.

My middle son, Landan, was sensitive and incredibly hard working from his early days. He loved sports and would do drills to the point of complete exhaustion. He has also always had an incredible insight into people. He sees what few others notice. He can sense what is going on in people. He would sense things about others when he was just a boy and he would be right. Talking with him about this over the years slowly increased his appreciation for who God made him to be. Today he celebrates his gifts and lives into them. Watch, discuss, honor, and celebrate who your kid is.

Logan, my youngest, has been secure since the day he was born. He does not look to others for his lead. He leads. When he was in third grade, he

"Celebrate your kid's unique interests, not yours."

EXPLORATION

63

mentioned to me one night as I was tucking him into bed that he got roughed up on the playground at school. I asked him who the boys were and assured him I had "friends" who would take care of them. He said he was playing on the parallel bar hanging upside down when four fifth-graders came over and told him that only little girls do that and he should stop. Logan swung down and leaned against the bar, and told them that he would play when and how he wanted. Way to go, little man! These four boys proceeded to rough my kid up as he clung to the playground equipment. They kicked and shoved him. I asked Logan why he did not just walk away and do something else. His answer says volumes about Logan. He told me, *"Dad, those guys can't tell me what to do."* There is a clue to who God has made Logan from that experience. The truth of what I learned about him that night continues today. Listen to your kid, assess what it means, give feedback, and celebrate his or her strengths.

"Remember to express interest without being nosey. Learn to press for understanding without being pushy."

Remember to express interest without being nosey. Learn to press for understanding without being pushy. At times our kids may resist us for one reason or another. They just may not be interested in having a conversation today. That is fine. Pushing will only lead to anger, and anger kills closeness. Closeness is a precious commodity in building the kind of trust that leads to insight and breakthrough. When it comes to talking about this stuff, it is better to back off when you sense resistance than to bruise the relationship. We do not want to wear a kid out dissecting his or her life. We want to lead kids to a place of gratitude for who God has made them to be.

AN EXPLORER'S HEART #4—LIVES IN THE TENSION OF NOT KNOWING THE MEANING OF IT ALL

Each of these experiences will be a snapshot of our kid. Over time they create an album of insights that reveal themes and patterns. It will take months and years to confirm and clarify little insights gained in any single experience. Kids are wet cement, and we don't want to see it harden by premature or unconfirmed observations. Along the way it is wise to ask God for the grace to live in the tension of *"I don't know yet, it's too early to tell."* This will often be your response to specific questions about who your kid is.

Landan, my middle son, has always been sensitive. All little boys are sensitive but he had a deep, tender side to him as a boy. I wondered what that meant. What would it mean for him vocationally up the road? Early on, neither of us was sure. It created heaps of pain for him. As a parent I suffered with him. He would feel things deeper than most, and that wasn't always fun. I'd tell him that God had given him his tender heart for a reason and just to trust that we would understand why in time. I would do everything I could to bless that part of him even when his brothers would make fun of it. We had many alone conversations where I'd have to remind him it is not just good, it is wonderful, that God had made him that way. He would look at me and tearfully ask, *"Why dad? Why am I like this?"* I would tell him, *"I don't know yet, it's too early to tell."*

Today we both know why. Today he deals with people in pain every day. Landan is a chiropractor. His ability to see into people and sense their conditions is stunning. Couple that perceptivity with his deep knowledge of the systems of the body, and you have a healer. Today, way up the road, it makes sense.

Work hard at looking through the Exploration window. Cheer your kid on to try things and pay attention to his or her reaction. Debrief those life experiences and accumulate insights. The *31-Day Experience* will offer additional first steps you can take. We will turn next to consider the most powerful force available for good in a kid's life...Affirmation.

" 'Why dad? Why am I like this?' I would tell him,
'I don't know yet, it's too early to tell.' "

Action Plan for the Exploration Window

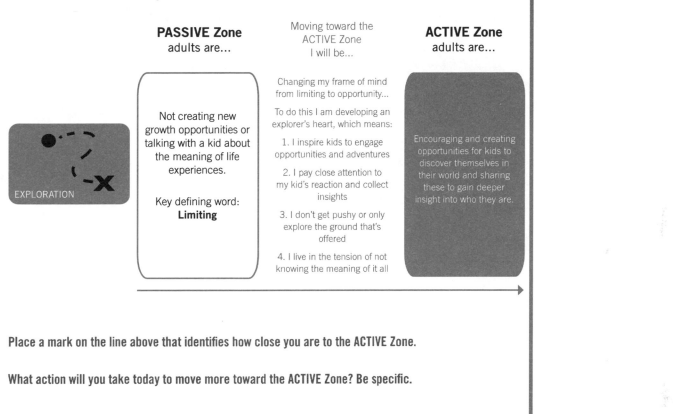

PASSIVE Zone
adults are...

Moving toward the
ACTIVE Zone
I will be...

ACTIVE Zone
adults are...

EXPLORATION

Not creating new
growth opportunities or
talking with a kid about
the meaning of life
experiences.

Key defining word:
Limiting

Changing my frame of mind
from limiting to opportunity...

To do this I am developing an
explorer's heart, which means:

1. I inspire kids to engage
opportunities and adventures

2. I pay close attention to
my kid's reaction and collect
insights

3. I don't get pushy or only
explore the ground that's
offered

4. I live in the tension of not
knowing the meaning of it all

Encouraging and creating
opportunities for kids to
discover themselves in
their world and sharing
these to gain deeper
insight into who they are.

Place a mark on the line above that identifies how close you are to the ACTIVE Zone.

What action will you take today to move more toward the ACTIVE Zone? Be specific.

What adult friend is inspiring you to stay at it as you participate in KidUnique? Be sure to thank them for their encouragement.

EXPLORATION

👍 **WHERE WE LOOK TO SEE KIDS**

Chapter Four

AFFIRMATION...the power of telling kids what's right with them

You will have to live with the consequences of everything you say. What you say can preserve life or destroy it; so you must accept the consequences of your words.

Proverbs 18:20-21 TEV

"Lord, let not one thought, one word, one attitude or one action be outside of your will today."

Daily prayer of Tom Paterson

AFFIRMATION: speaking the upside truth to kids...communicating what is right with them

I awakened to the power of affirmation when I was in 10th grade. I entered high school as a sophomore weighing 185 pounds while being only 5'5" tall. I would roll from one class to the other. Life was painful and insecurity dominated me like a mean older brother. Two questions drifted regularly in and out of my mind. The first was—*am I lovable?* The second was—*do I have what it takes?*

Even though I was overweight, I tried out for every sports team. I'm not sure why. I didn't make a single team and the shame of being cut only intensified the questioning of my worth and ability. Thank God for Dr. David Messenger.

Dr. Messenger was my 10th-grade algebra teacher and the coach of the boys' sophomore basketball team. At the end of tryouts he called me over and suggested I consider managing the team. I said, *"Sure coach, and after that I'll go home and kiss my sister!"* It just wasn't my idea of a good time. He responded by offering me the possibility of earning extra credit in algebra class. I asked, *"How much extra credit?"* He made me an offer I couldn't refuse. As a result, every afternoon you'd find me out with the sophomore basketball team assisting the coach and occasionally participating in practice when a kid would be hurt or sick. After the last practice of the year Dr. Messenger told me to bag up the balls and see him before I went home. What was said during that conversation changed the course of my life.

Dr. Messenger said he had two things to say to me. The first was that he was grateful for my help all season. He assured me that I would get my extra credit and sincerely thanked me for my service to the team. He said he couldn't have done it without me. Nice words, and I heard him. Then he made an observation that changed my life. He said, *"Dan, you should go out for basketball next year. I believe there is a varsity athlete in you."* I almost passed out. He could not mean that. Was this another cruel joke? I kept waiting for the punch line but it never came. My bewildered response was... "*Really?*" He went on to say, "*All season long you have helped with practice and often jumped in and played to cover for one of the guys who was injured. As you practiced with the team I noticed something...you have more athletic ability than any kid on this team. You just haven't grown up yet. You haven't hit your growth spurt. Once you do, you will see that there is a varsity basketball player in you.*" I was stunned. I could barely speak. His words changed my life.

During the following summer Mother Nature hit me with her wand and I had a growth spurt. Because of the power of Dr. Messenger's words, along with being 6 inches taller, I rallied the courage to try out for basketball. Guess what? Dr. Messenger was right. I made the team and was co-captain of the junior varsity that year. The following year I played on a varsity team that went to the state championship game in the Los Angeles Sports Arena. I often wonder what would have happened if Dr. Messenger hadn't spoken those words to me. If he would have stayed silent and only thought about affirming my potential, I would never have gone out for basketball. God bless Dr. David Messenger for speaking up.

AFFIRMATION...SPEAKING THE UPSIDE TRUTH TO A KID

The Affirmation window turns loose a potentially transforming power. It has the potential to unleash a kid's gifts upon the world and unlocks the God-given extraordinary. You are going to fuel your kid's future success through affirmation. Few things are as life affecting. Every day your kid lives with the same two questions that haunted me in high school. *Am I lovable?* and *Do I have what it takes?* Affirmation answers both questions.

Affirmation is telling your kid what's right with him or her. It is being a big enough person and having a strong enough love to see beyond what is wrong and point out what's right. It is noticing, and then communicating verbally, the upside truth of who he or she is and the talents God has provided.

Tom Paterson is my true Yoda. He is a famous business consultant, mentor, and source of wisdom to many, including me. For over 40 years he consulted

"*The Affirmation window turns loose a potentially transforming power. It has the potential to unleash a kid's gifts upon the world and unlocks the God-given extraordinary.*"

for Fortune 500 companies. During those years he worked with some amazing marketplace leaders. Recently Tom made a comment that I still have trouble getting my head around. He said, *"Dan, over all my years of working with business leaders I've never met a man who, once I got to know him, didn't have a streak of insecurity running through his life because of an absence of affirmation when he was young."* I found that hard to believe. Tom has worked with some incredibly successful and powerful men. I told him he had to be overstating his case. He smiled and quietly repeated, *"Maybe you didn't hear me. As I've worked with leaders over all the years I've never met a man who, once I got to know him, didn't have a streak of insecurity running through his life because of an absence of affirmation when he was young."* He insisted that it was true. Upon deeper reflection, I have come to agree with Yoda.

Why is this true? Why is it that our kids seem to be infected with a low-grade fever of insecurity and inferiority? It is because they live in a world of comparison and often only see *who they aren't* instead of *who they are.* This is incredibly toxic to self-esteem. Comparison points out the strengths of others, highlighting what we don't have compared to them. That is trouble. The constant pressure of comparison can kill self-esteem. It killed mine when I was in middle school and high school.

I also believe that kids have low confidence because the majority of feedback they get is either inaccurate or solely focused on what's wrong with them. Kids need us to tell them what's right with them. The pressure of "living up to" the expectations others have for them can get burdensome. KidUnique is about inspiring kids to "live into" the people God has created them to be. There is a difference. They need us to recognize and communicate truth about who they are in a way that lifts them above the negativity of the world they live in. Oh, for a few KidUnique adults who cut through all the fog layers of a kid's insecurity with the penetrating power of kind and truthful words!

GOD LOVES AFFIRMATION

Jesus affirmed his close followers. He went out of his way to call a few people close to him for special training. Being chosen as the focus of his

the slowest kid in my grade

no one would miss me

no one will play with me

I'm fat and stupid

feel different from others

I hate my life right now

"Why is it that our kids seem to be infected with a low-grade fever of insecurity and inferiority? It is because they live in a world of comparison and often only see who they aren't instead of who they are."

love and training was incredibly affirming. You have chosen a kid as the focus of your attention. That is a clear statement of love.

Jesus often lifted the vision of his followers to help them see who they were and who they could be. You will do this for a kid, too. He convinced them that they could become difference makers in the lives of others—*"I will show you how to fish for people" (Mark 1:17).*

Jesus went out of his way to call the disciples his friends—*"Now you are my friends..." (John 15:15).* That's a wonderfully uplifting statement that brought joy to the disciples. Your kid is going to feel the warmth of your friendship.

Jesus even looked a young leader named Peter in the face and told him he was a rock and that God's church would be built on his broad shoulders. *"Now I say to you that you are Peter (which means 'rock'), and upon this rock I will build my church, and all the powers of hell will not conquer it" (Matthew 16:18).* We will work hard to see and name talents and strength in our kids and call them to live into them.

Ultimately Jesus' greatest affirmation was to lay down his life for them. *"There is no greater love than to lay down one's life for one's friends" (John 15:13).* Every time you listen, care, share, and lift your kid you are laying your life down. Simply stated: Jesus understood what it meant to look through the Affirmation window, and he modeled living in the power of it.

Pause a moment. Before we move ahead, reread what it means to be in the ACTIVE zone as it applies to the Affirmation window. Do not forget that the goal is to always be moving from left to right in our thinking and behaviors.

PASSIVE Zone behavior toward a kid	Moving toward the ACTIVE Zone = changing my mindset	ACTIVE Zone behavior toward a kid
AFFIRMATION		
I am too negative and point out only what's wrong with my kid.	I am engaging AFFIRMATION when I shift my frame of mind from the mess to the miracle...	I am constantly watching for and telling kids what's right about them. I seek out positive gossip concerning them. AFFIRMATION is alive and well

How do we affirm our kids?

The work of affirmation is about spending the energy to both pay attention to and think about your kid so that you can identify his or her upside and then form meaningful and uplifting communication strategies. Here are three simple ways to affirm.

Say It

Few things are as uplifting for a kid as hearing positive truthful words spoken in ways that touch the very core. King Solomon understood this: *A cheerful look brings joy to the heart; good news makes for good health (Proverbs 15:30).* We all feel better when we hear good news about who we are.

Saying something true and uplifting does not cost you a penny but is worth its weight in gold. *The speech of a good person is worth waiting for; the blabber of the wicked is worthless (Proverbs 10:20 The Message).* We want kids to look forward to times with us. We want them to be confident in the fact that our words will be positive and uplifting. Make sure your weekly touches have moments of affirmation. Do not forget these. In those moments, say the things you have seen in them or heard others say about them. This is what looking through the Affirmation window is all about.

Affirmation is noticing any small place of potential or personal growth in a kid and blessing it. Look for attitudes, deeds, or accomplishments. Notice sacrifices, good actions taken, efforts made in the right direction and point them out. Identify what you specifically want to affirm, then grab the kid and

"Few things are as uplifting for a kid as hearing positive truthful words spoken in ways that touch the very core."

Think of what you can affirm in your kid right now. Write these down.

Affirmation #1

Affirmation #2

Affirmation #3

say, *"Hey, I have been meaning to tell you something for a while ..."* It is that easy.

Affirmation is not blowing sunshine at a kid. It is not lying or just blabbing fluffy happy thoughts. It is not shielding him or her from the tough feedback life brings that must be heard. It is trying to see into a kid and point out who he or she is, what gifts God has given, and the person he or she can become.

Over the years I have gone face-to-face with the kids I love and made statements like...

> *"I'm proud of the way you owned your wrong and apologized. That says great things about you."*

> *"Way to be honest on that test. I know you could have cheated but you chose to live with a clear conscience. Nice job."*

> *"You've been working hard in the weight room haven't you? You look great."*

> *"You stayed up late last night studying, didn't you? That's good stuff."*

> *"You showed your inner strength and trust in God when you decided not to go out with that guy. That was a smart decision."*

> *"You didn't do the beat-down on your younger brother when you could have last night. Thanks for being kind to him; I won't tell your friends about it."*

> *"You really went out of your way to help that guy. That was incredible."*

> *"You should go to college. You are smart and hardworking."*

"You are a courageous person. Your dad has been a jerk but you choose to love him anyway. Way to go."

"You gave away your last $5 to your friend, didn't you? Boy, that was generous of you."

It is just that simple. It will take courage, time, and initiative. You can do this!

Write It

Over the years I have written hundreds of notes to the people I care about and kids I have mentored. It never ceases to amaze me the impact they have. Years later kids who are now adults tell me they have kept the notes and reread them during tough times. That should not surprise me because I do the same with affirmative notes I have received. I understand today that hearing a verbal *"I love you"* does not stick like a written reminder. When life is caving in and a kid wonders if he or she matters to anyone, a note or two from you is a great reminder. Remember that there is nothing like a letter that puts into a permanent form something that is right about a kid.

Here is a note I wrote to a KidUnique adult I greatly admire. She shows up every day as a middle school teacher and helps kids discover who they are. I love her for that. She works with kids who have learning disabilities. Most of them have lousy self-esteem. She is a one-woman affirmation band that plays the sweet music of God's love to kids.

One of those kids was my middle son. She helped him years ago when he was in seventh and eighth grades. She did all the things someone should do to express love and confidence to a kid. She literally saved his academic life by teaching him strategies to address his reading disability. The note you will read is the third I sent to her over a number of years. It, along with her response, illustrates the power of affirmation.

Hey Susanne...what's goin' on? This December will be an exciting month for the Webster household. It should also be an exciting month for you.

Why, you ask? Here's why. One of your former students who suffered under some real learning challenges has found the determination and courage to live into his potential. One kid who sat with you in seventh and eighth grades and chose to listen to you and take your instruction to heart will realize a dream that he once thought way beyond his reach. One young man who believed it when you told him, 'Hey, buddy, you're plenty smart, we just have to find some ways to help you,' will stand before his professors, fellow students, and family and receive a doctor of chiropractic degree.

Shoot dang Susanne...a doctorate. I can't even spell the word. Wow, does that fill my heart with both joy and gratitude. You know that I gave thanks to God for you at Landan's high school and college graduations. Well, I just thought I'd let you know there will be a prayer of, 'yipee-stinken-dodah-bless-the-Lord-God-Almighty-for-Susanne' descending from this dad's heart during that ceremony, too.

You are the best, Susanne. Stay tender and surrendered to God and keep bringing 'it' daily to your kids. And as God gives you strength...give them your best. Never forget that I both love and believe in you. Now, go tear it up today! Spread your life-changing God-inspired love around because there's some kid who needs you.

Grateful –

Dan

Susanne's response...

Thanks for all your encouragement over the years. I have your most recent letter in the kitchen where I can pick it up and read it as needed. Last year was a bad year...I told everyone I knew that I was retiring. The truth is, I am too young to retire; I was quitting. Your letter arrived at God's time. God confirmed the words in the letter as words I still say to my students. So, thank you for encouraging me. I'm back on track and having the time of my life, teaching and telling kids that they can.

I am proud of Landan for listening to his cheerleaders, for believing in finding his own way to learn, for perseverance in the daily academic tasks that brought him to that place that God had in mind all those years ago. Congrats to you too, for seeing his potential and believing in him and standing with him all the way!

Thanks for investing time to keep me encouraged and updated all these years.

And, yes, God is good.

Susanne

Affirmative notes do not need to be dramatic or complex. They can be brief or funny. I once received a note that was written on toilet paper. This is what my creative friend wrote on the toilet paper to affirm me.

Dear Dan, I really like this toilet paper. It is cusssssssh, and it's soft—much like you in your dealings with delicate human lives. Also, like this toilet paper you are so good at wiping up messy and awkward situations. And you're always right there, ready to be used. Yes Dan, I'd say you're just the toilet paper of God in a world of crap.

I still smile every time I think about that ridiculous note.

I will often shoot a text message to one of my sons reminding him that I carry him in my heart. I believe if my sons know their dad is with them, really with them, their lives will be a bit easier. Recently I sent Logan this text message, *"Logan—dad here—just wanted you to know that whatever comes your way today, good or bad, easy or hard...your dad loves you."* Pretty simple, huh? Your kid needs to know you are with him or her—so say it often, in writing.

Who can you talk with this week that may be able to share some positive gossip concerning the kid you love? Write their names below:

Positive gossip source #1

What they said about my kid:

Positive gossip source #2

What they said about my kid:

Positive gossip source #3

What they said about my kid:

Seek Positive Gossip

How do you think your kid would react if you said: *"Hey, I heard so and so talking about you and they said...?"* 90 percent of the time a kid's gut reaction will be to wonder what trash might have been said about him or her. How freaked out might they be if they heard that the words spoken behind their backs were positive? We know the power of negative gossip. The Bible warns us of how people can use words to destroy. *Scoundrels create trouble; their words are a destructive blaze (Proverbs 16:27).*

One of your jobs is to chase down positive gossip about your kid. You are not alone in your task of helping a kid discover who he or she is. Teachers, coaches, family members, youth pastors, and others know and care about your kid. Ask these people for insight into the positive things they see.

A couple of months ago I made a presentation to the faculty and administration of the local Christian school district. At the conclusion of my talk, Mrs. Berry, a teacher, came up to me and said, *"I had your sons in my class when I was teaching at the public high school years ago. I loved each one of them, especially Luke. How is he doing?"*

This is a nice bit of positive gossip. Luke heard about my conversation with Mrs. Berry before the day was over. I am always listening for others who are lifting my sons up behind their backs. Throughout their lives I have passed along any positive words others have spoken. Coaches and teachers have said positive things to me about my sons that they would not say directly to them. Whenever I hear these words, you can be sure they get passed on.

As you practice passing on positive gossip, you will learn what King Solomon knew: *Good news from far away is like cold water to the thirsty (Proverbs 25:25).* Every kid's soul gets thirsty for the good news of affirmation, whether it comes through words spoken to his or her face, in written form, or through the surprise of positive gossip.

Realize also that as you affirm a kid you will be answering those two lingering questions...

Am I lovable? Through your affirmation you are telling them, *"Yes, yes, a thousands times yes. I am here, I am expressing love...you are lovable. Listen to my words. They tell you that you matter."*

Do I have what it takes? When you affirm a kid and tell who he or she is on the upside you are saying, *"Yes you have what it takes! Every right thing about you that I identify and pass on will remind you of that. Believe these things and live into them."*

As we end this chapter on the Affirmation window, settle in your heart that every time you connect with your kid, affirmation will be a part of the conversation. Determine that you will have something to tell that is true on the upside. The *31-Day Experience* will offer practical ideas for how to look through the Affirmation window. Before we get to that, let's move on to consider the Revelation window and ponder God's involvement in this process.

AFFIRMATION

Action Plan for the Affirmation Window

PASSIVE Zone
adults are...

Moving toward the
ACTIVE Zone
I will be...

ACTIVE Zone
adults are...

AFFIRMATION

Chronically negative,
pointing out only what's
wrong with a kid.

Key defining word:
Negative

Adjusting my frame of mind
from the mess to the miracle.

Learning to affirm my kid more
means:

1. I speak affirmation to my kid

2. I write notes of affirmation

3. I seek out positive gossip

Constantly watching for and
telling kids what is right with
them and seeking out positive
gossip concerning a kid.

When this happens...
AFFIRMATION

Place a mark on the line above that identifies how close you are to the ACTIVE Zone.

What action will you take today to move more toward the ACTIVE Zone? Be specific.

What adult friend have you asked to pray for you as you participate in KidUnique? Call them and give them an update on how things are going.

 **WHERE WE LOOK TO SEE KIDS**

Chapter Five
REVELATION...the power of listening to God in the process

I will instruct you and teach you in the way which you should go;
I will counsel you with My eye upon you.

Psalm 32:8 NASB

This is what God said: "Before I shaped you in the womb,
I knew all about you. Before you saw the light of day,
I had holy plans for you..."

Jeremiah 1:4-5 The Message

Revelation: God speaking to people in the context of human history

August 1, 1998, was a great day in the life of former Chicago Bears all-pro middle linebacker Mike Singletary. It was the day this two-time league defensive MVP and Super Bowl champion was inducted into the National Football League Hall of Fame. I remember watching Mike's acceptance speech on ESPN2 with two of my sons that Saturday afternoon. True to Mike's personality, he was both intense and passionate. He generously thanked God, his family members, friends, former coaches, and teammates for the support they had offered over the years. But the most powerful and heartfelt comments Mike made that day were about his mother and a conversation they had when he was only 12. Their conversation offers light as we learn how to look through the Revelation window and help our kids discover who they are. Without Rudell Singletary's words to Mike, he may never have found his way. Below is the beginning to Mike's Hall of Fame induction speech (profootballhof.com). Pay close attention to the words his mother spoke to him.

This story began a long way back—Houston, Texas. Sort of began when I was 12 years old because there were a lot of things happening at that particular time in my family. We were going through a lot, we were trying to go to the next level. And I am the last of 10 kids and when you have 10 kids, sometimes it's a little bit of a struggle to make it work. That year when I was 12 years old mom and dad went through a divorce. When I was 5 years old my brother Dale passed away and my second brother would pass away when I was age 12. That was a tough year, I had no confidence, had no self-esteem. Just a young ghetto boy in Houston, Texas, trying to figure out who he was and where he was going to go from there. And I want to tell you today my mom, my mom sat me down one day when I was moping around and feeling sorry for myself, close to giving up. I began listening to everybody else in the neighborhood who said, 'No one gets out of here. No one has ever made it out of here and you won't either. Besides, you don't have the ability, you don't have the skill, you don't have anything.' My mom sat me down that day and she let me know something that I always knew but, man, I needed to hear it. Mom sat me down and said, 'Son, I want you to know something.' She said, 'I want you to know that there is greatness in you, there's something special about you. I prayed for you before you were born and every day since. It's in there! You've got to find it for yourself. I'm going to do everything I can as a mother to get it there but you've got to find it.' She put her hands on my forearm and she asked me if I could become the man around the house. I said, 'Mom I can do that.' That day I went to my room and I wrote down my goals. And at 12 years old it went something like this: find a way to get a scholarship to go to college, become an All-American in college, get my degree, go to the NFL and buy my mom a house and take care of her for the rest of my life.*

At 12 years old the great Mike Singletary *"had no confidence, no self-esteem...just a ghetto boy in Houston, Texas trying to figure out who he was and where he was going...close to giving up."* Lucky for Mike he had a mother who was tougher than he would ever be. Her courage, passion, determination, prayers, and words saved his life and helped him see into the future.

Rudell Singletary did what KidUnique adults do. She envisioned who her kid might be. She believed he had God-given potential. She would do anything to fight for his extraordinary life. She prayed every day that Mike would come to know what he was made for and that he would find his way and live into his greatness. Rudell longed for a touch of the divine in the discovery process and got it. Let's follow in her brave footsteps.

IT'S A SPIRITUAL THING

The very task of KidUnique is spiritual in nature. We can't dodge this fact. From the day our kids were conceived there has been far more going on than just meets the eye. KidUnique adults believe that God made their kids, knows them better, and loves them deeper than they ever could. KidUnique adults believe that God wants to help with this process.

Ultimately we understand that kids must ask God for his will concerning who they are and what they should do with their lives. As Rudell told Mike, *"You've got to find it for yourself...I'm going to do everything I can as a mother to get*

"At 12 years old the great Mike Singletary 'had no confidence, no self-esteem... just a ghetto boy in Houston, Texas trying to figure out who he was and where he was going...close to giving up.' Lucky for Mike he had a mother who was tougher than he would ever be."

"The very task of KidUnique is spiritual in nature.
We can't dodge this fact. From the day our kids were
conceived there has been far more going on than
just meets the eye."

it there but you've got to find it." We love, we "see," we lift, we interact, we pray, but in the end they must listen to God and engage, too. She knew Mike would need a spark of God's confirmation along the way. Learning to look through the Revelation window is about accessing the help of God with this task. It begins with me saying to God, *"I need your help. I can't do this alone."*

I am not sure where you stand today concerning the "God thing." This is not a book debating the merits for the existence of God or about trying to persuade you to "get saved." You may already be a fully devoted follower of God or you may only be engaging the KidUnique project because you want to help your kid find the way into the future. Maybe you are warm to the idea of God or maybe not. I settled the "God thing" in my life years ago when I surrendered to him on a summer night in Southern California, while standing on third base in Angel Stadium in Anaheim at a Billy Graham Crusade. I heard the good news about Jesus that evening and responded. I told God I would gladly receive his outrageous gift of forgiveness and grace offered in his Son Jesus Christ. Since that night I have been re-surrendering daily while learning to trust God, walk in his ways and accomplish what I believe is his work assigned to me. For 30 years as a dad I have also been gladly receiving his help in the work of KidUnique. I can't imagine facing this task without God's help.

IS THERE DIVINE HELP? JOHN THE WHO...?

Can you imagine what it would be like to have an angel appear from heaven and tell you both who your kid is and what God's will is for his or her life? That is what happened to the parents of a famous biblical character named John the Baptist. John's mother, Elizabeth, was advancing in years and unable to bear children. She had prayed about this issue countless times with her husband, Zacharias. An angel of the Lord appeared to him one day and announced that God had heard his petition and his wife would bear a son. That must have been a shocker. Read slowly what the angel tells Zacharias will be true of John. These words were spoken even before the kid was conceived. Think about what it would be like to hear these words and one day be

"This is not a book debating the merits for the existence of God or about trying to persuade you to 'get saved.' "

responsible to communicate them to your kid. Take a pen and underline the phrases in the passage that reveal who John would be.

"...you are to name him John. You will have great joy and gladness, and many will rejoice at his birth, for he will be great in the eyes of the Lord. He must never touch wine or other alcoholic drinks. He will be filled with the Holy Spirit, even before his birth. And he will turn many Israelites to the Lord their God. He will be a man with the spirit and power of Elijah. He will prepare the people for the coming of the Lord. He will turn the hearts of the fathers to their children, and he will cause those who are rebellious to accept the wisdom of the godly" (Luke 1:13-17).

That is quite a prophecy spoken by the angel concerning the unborn John. What a windfall for Zacharias and Elizabeth to receive clear data from the Deity concerning their son's identity. John had a unique destiny. I wonder how many conversations Elizabeth and Zacharias had about the angel visitation.

> *"His clothing was camel's hair and a leather belt. Sounds like a kid who might have had some 'issues' early on."*

Think about your kid for a moment. What would it be like if an angel from heaven showed up and said, *"Hey, let me help you with this KidUnique stuff. God has told me who he made your kid to be."*

I have often wondered when Elizabeth and Zacharias broke the news to young John about the angel's visitation before his birth. How did John receive that news and the calling that would be his? How early and how deep was his sense of God's calling on his life? Did John celebrate the news from his parents or resist it? Did he give his parents a dirty look and say, *"You've got to be kidding me? Forerunner? No way. I was considering becoming a dentist or a farmer or an artist."* We don't know.

What we do know is that somewhere along the line John moved to the wilderness and lived alone eating insects and wild honey. His clothing was camel's hair and a leather belt (Mark 1:6). Sounds like a kid who might have had some "issues" early on. We also know from Scripture that it was in the wilderness where the word of the Lord came to him and confirmed both his calling and the angel's words.

I love the fact that John was capable of hearing the voice of God and that God was more than able to communicate to him. There came a time when John did not need Mom and Dad to hold his hand. God often speaks to kids in spite of moms and dads, and for that I am grateful. One day God did speak and John responded. I am sure John was grateful for the faith foundation his parents laid. Once God spoke, John got on board and began living into the life God had for him. As he did, John experienced what King David mentions in Psalm 139:14 NASB, *I will give thanks to You, for I am fearfully and wonderfully made; wonderful are Your works, and my soul knows it very well.* John's soul knew who he was and what God's will was for his life...his soul knew it very well.

Daily I long for my soul to know very well that I am made by God, wonderful and gifted for a purpose. I long for my kids to know that, too. Stating this desire seems easy. It contains a powerful longing that lives within me. But it is a challenge to get there. Thanks to this wonderful dance between John, his parents, and the angel, John was able to understand, believe, and follow God's will for his life—and the rest is history. I am sure there were plenty of opportunities to step on each other's toes in the dance to discover John's destiny.

Pause a moment. Before we consider John's story, reread what it means to be in the ACTIVE zone as it applies to the Revelation window. Do not forget that the goal is to always be moving from left to right in our thinking and behavior.

PASSIVE Zone behavior toward a kid	Moving toward the ACTIVE Zone = changing my mindset	ACTIVE Zone behavior toward a kid
REVELATION		
I am prayer-less, defeated, fearful, frustrated, and not trusting or believing God can speak or help.	I am engaging REVELATION when I shift my frame of mind from frustration to prayer and listening...	I daily pray for wisdom, trust God and listen for promptings all through the process **REVELATION** is experienced

Listening Lessons

KidUnique adults understand the importance of the Revelation window even though they may not be able to articulate what it is with great clarity. There is something elusive and mysterious about hearing from God and talking about it with your kid. How do you say, *"I think I might have a sense of who God has made you to be."* without sounding a little...well, wacky?

Rudell Singletary risked sounding wacky to Mike, and he is glad she took that risk. It helped point him into his future. We should not allow this concern to be an excuse to shy away from the topic or ignore the need for Revelation in our kids' lives.

God wants to speak to your kid and you get to be a part of it. To help us gain some additional clarity on the issue of heavenly communication, let us learn a lesson or two from the story of John the Baptist. Rudell lived these lessons out with her son Mike and we can follow her example.

Lesson One: Heavenly communication comes most easily to those who listen

The first lesson has to do with the fact that John the Baptist's parents were spiritual people. This seems a bit obvious but let's state it anyway. They believed in God's ability to speak. As a result they recognized the presence of divine communication and believed it.

I'm not sure where you stand on this issue. You may not believe God speaks to normal folks like us. I know I am cautious and skeptical about much of what I hear people say is communication from God. There are many who are not discerning and think they hear communication from heaven when it is only wishful thinking or their own thoughts. Caution is in order as we approach the Revelation window. This is why it is important that we mature spiritually. I never want to glibly toss out a *"God said to me..."* statement to a kid. At the same time, kids need for us to live in close communication with God and say what we may sense he is communicating.

"There are many who are not discerning and think they hear communication from heaven when it is only wishful thinking or their own thoughts."

How did John the Baptist get a vision for becoming John the Baptist? It was through the words of his dad, Zacharias, who heard it from the angel. Up the road God confirmed those words to John personally, and he lived into them. I am sure there were moments during John's early years in the wake of a childhood failure or temper tantrum when his parents had to wonder, *"Are you sure, God? Forerunner? Turn the hearts of the fathers back to the children? Really?"* But they hung with John, believed, and were patient as he grew up.

How did Mike Singletary dare to believe that there might be some greatness in him? It was through the words of a God-honoring mom. How did she know that there was greatness in Mike? I would guess two things contributed. First, she prayed for Mike and as she did she got a sense about Mike. The second was that she had a history of watching the kid play around the house hundreds of times and listening to him talk about life every day. From those relational connects and her quiet heart before God, I believe she got a sense from God who Mike was at his core. The same will be true for us.

You may be thinking, *"Shoot, I'm no Zacharias or Rudell."* Maybe not yet, but do not wimp out on this. Be motivated by the fact that our spiritual sensitivity and depth will assist us in being able to hear God's voice and/or confirm his communication to our kids. This means the best thing we can do for our kids is to walk closely with God and learn to hear his promptings and voice. I have written about this in detail in other places.[14]

A Powerful Prayer

One thing I have done to keep my eye on the ball when it comes to praying for my kids is to write out a prayer for them (and me). I come back to this prayer often, whenever I begin to feel a loss of hope or perspective, and it reminds me which end is up. In the *31-Day Experience* you will have the opportunity to write such a prayer for yourself and your kid.

Father, thank you for your unending love and patience with me and my sons. Right now this KidUnique responsibility feels too much for me without your help. I can't do it alone. I affirm in this moment of frustration that you made my sons. You know them better than they know themselves. You have invested gifts, talents, and interests in them. I know you love them far more than I could ever love them. I know you see them every second of the day. I know you are the one who can bring insight and meaning to all my son's daily experiences. I know you can care for them with or without me. This I believe, Lord, this I know.

As I sit before you now, I thank you (by faith) for the privilege of serving them. I'm asking for insight to recognize the 'heavenly messengers' You send to help show the way. I need more than me and my wisdom. I'm not smart or insightful enough to help them without your help. At times I feel blind as I observe them. Open my eyes, God, to see them as you see them. At times I'm resentful of the opportunities they have. Enlarge my heart to celebrate and create more for them.

Lift me, God, to bless the miracle that they are and not only remind them of the mess of their lives. Please speak to me as the angel spoke to Zacharias. Let your word come to my sons as it came to John in the wilderness. Protect my kids with your power. Grace me with the love and wisdom to assist them as we listen to you for their future. Be powerful here, Lord. I am trusting you 100 percent with this task. Amen.

Lesson Two: Don't be surprised if your kid receives heavenly communication

The second lesson is that John was also capable of hearing God's voice. Don't ever think you have the only pipeline to God. Our kids can hear God. The best person to know whether God is speaking to your kid is your kid. What kids need is confirmation from us that it may indeed be God speaking.

Is this true of you?

"I'm fully convinced that God has created me for a particular purpose in life that will bring glory to him."

Agree ------ 89.9%
Disagree --- 10.1%

From GROUP Magazine's annual survey of over 30,000 Christian teenagers. Sept/Oct 2009 - Volume 35

God spoke to John the Baptist, and he heard God. There will be times when your kid will both hear and understand that God is speaking. There will be many other times when you will need to discern and talk about the "heavenly communication" God is sending his or her way. God speaks to the young. Often they are more attentive to his voice and promptings than we are.

A daring, but important, question to ask your kid is, *"Have you sensed God saying anything to you about you or your future?"* Ask it sometime. If your kid says "yes" just listen and don't judge or react. If he or she responds with a "not sure" or "no," encourage an openness toward listening for God's voice.

I had a sense from the age of 18 that God wanted to use me in a powerful way. I was not sure exactly where or how. That came with time, but I felt it in my soul. I don't remember anyone asking me if I had a sense from God about my future or if God had spoken to me. I didn't know who to talk to about what I was hearing. Who do you share that with? The result was that I deeply questioned myself and wondered whether God's whispers were real and true. I had to fight for my extraordinary life in those early days of following God. I believe God is speaking to kids today and they desperately need a God-trusting adult to say, *"Believe it kid...you have a huge future."*

God did encourage me many times through those early years. He used people who were spiritual enough and courageous enough to share little divine whispers they had concerning me. Over the years I have had people say, *"God nudged me to tell you to keep working on your teaching gift because he is going to use that big time...you are a serious kingdom player, I can sense it, stay faithful, kid...you have the shots to make a real difference, others listen to you...I sense you have leadership abilities that God will greatly use..."* Every time one of those statements came my way, someone was looking through the Revelation window, and it fired up the faith within me.

I remember one of the pastors at the church I was serving telling me years after I had built and led a very successful student ministry, "Dan, I always sensed you had a grand destiny and that God was going to use you." My response was, *"Why didn't you tell me back then? I could have used the encouragement. You have no idea how much I doubted myself."* He said, *"I'm sorry, I didn't know you ever struggled. You always seemed confident."* With a little more intensity than I should have, I said to him, *"Listen, in the future if you EVER get a nudge or whisper from God about a kid as it relates to who he or she is and a possible destiny, SAY IT!"*

I would say the same to you. Do not underestimate the power of telling a kid an insight that you believe God has given. Every one of us needs to be constantly reminded that God loves us and is favorable toward us. We all need to be Rudells.

We are almost ready to launch the *31-Day Experience*. There is only one other important issue to consider. For some of us, this issue is the ball game. Read carefully the next chapter and think honestly about the challenge it carries.

Action Plan for the Revelation Window

REVELATION

PASSIVE Zone
adults are...

Prayer-less, defeated, fearful, frustrated, and not trusting or believing God can speak or help.

Key defining word:
Alone

Moving toward the ACTIVE Zone
I will be...

Shifting my frame of mind from frustration to listening.

As I do this I am applying the two listening lessons, believing:

1. heavenly communication comes most easily to those who listen

2. my kid can receive heavenly communication and I'm praying that they do

ACTIVE Zone
adults are...

Daily praying for wisdom asking God to help in the process and listening for promptings all along the way.

Envisioning who this kid might be.

When I am praying, listening, and trusting **REVELATION** is in play.

Place a mark on the line above that identifies how close you are to the ACTIVE Zone.

What action will you take today to move more toward the ACTIVE Zone? Be specific.

What KidUnique adult is inspiring you as you continue in this sacred task? Call them and ask them to keep praying for you.

FROM TALK TO WALK—
MAKING IT HAPPEN

Chapter Six
Resentment Assessment and the Invitation
...the power of eliminating obstacles

Fools have no interest in understanding;
they only want to air their own opinions.

Proverbs 18:2

Instead, be kind to each other, tenderhearted, forgiving one
another, just as God through Christ has forgiven you.

Ephesians 4:32

ASSESSMENT

Resentment: bitter indignation at having been treated unfairly

ELIMINATING OBSTACLES

My oldest son was 15 when he got arrested for possession of marijuana as a high school sophomore[15]. That was a painful day for the entire Webster household. We all felt sick to our stomachs, embarrassed, and confused. My relationship with Luke had fallen into a state of disrepair. I look back now and know that if I would have tried to cheerfully snuggle up to Luke and invite him into the process described in this book, he would have most likely flipped me off and walked away bubbling over with resentment. Things were not good, and I knew I had some obstacles to remove if I was to authentically reconnect with my oldest son.

That was an incredibly confusing and painful time as a parent. I wish I could tell you I was able to reconnect with Luke quickly. The truth is it took two years. That is right, two years. I did not know what to do as a dad during that time. The fact is, I was lost as a parent. I just was not mature enough or man enough or whatever enough to resolve things. When Luke was 17, and threatening to move out of the house, I invited him to a coffee shop to talk. We were going to try to sort things out. He sat silently looking at me with his arms crossed, and I knew he was mad. I was sure some of the anger was focused at himself. He had messed up and he knew it. Some was misdirected at the school administration. I could not do much about those sources of anger, but I decided that I could address one source...the anger he had toward me.

I decided to wade in and ask a few questions. I said to him, *"Luke, I'm not sure all that is going on with us or how we have gotten in this mess. I know it is gonna take us some time to figure it out. What I want you to know is that I am still your dad and I love you. So let's do what we haven't done for a while, talk honestly with one another. If you are willing, tell me how have I let you down. Say to me whatever you need to say. Do it unedited."*

He replied, *"Dad, you don't want to hear what I have to say."* I told him that was probably true but to go ahead and say it anyway and I would listen. What he said knocked the wind out of me. It was painful and honest. Luke has always been the most honest of my sons. He does not lie or pretend. Knowing that, I should have been ready for what he was about to say. I wasn't. The first few sentences out of his mouth were, *"Dad, every time you've talked to me in the last six months, you talk down to me...you make me feel guilty just by looking at me. I'm so f#*%ing tired of being the son of a perfect father I want to puke. If you knew the darkness that's in my heart you wouldn't even want me to be your son."* It went on from there.

He said what had to be said, and I did the best I could to listen. It would have been easy to power up, shame him, or just explode in frustration. If I had, we would have just fallen deeper into a dark hole. This was not about winning an argument; it was about recovering my relationship with my son. All of what came out during our conversation wasn't perfectly accurate or true. It never is in moments when emotions are high. He spoke and I listened. What he said was what he was feeling at the time.

We were not able to sort it all out over coffee that afternoon. We spent the months following that day in various states of disconnect. At times I struggled to have the maturity to listen. Other times, I just did not want to deal with it. The situation called for me to grow, and for a while I did not want to. The most important thing was to work hard at reestablishing the core of our relationship. Without that, we were done, and I refused to accept that option.

It was not easy sorting through his stuff and my stuff. But over time it got done. I asked him to forgive me for the hurt I had caused him and he gave me another chance...and another...and another. I forgave him, too. In that process I both owned and apologized for my part. He had to own his. With time he was able to own his side, and our relationship moved to a place of love and understanding. He let me back in, and I walked cautiously as we engaged about his life and future.

> *"This was not about winning an argument; it was about recovering my relationship with my son."*

"Dad, every time you've talked to me in the last six month, you talk down to me...you make me feel guilty just by looking at me. I'm so f#*%ing tired of being the son of a perfect father I want to puke. If you knew the darkness that's in my heart you wouldn't even want me to be your son."

That was a very important and fragile time in our relationship. Much of what has happened since then has been built upon the foundation we laid when he was 17 and in a rough place.

To let you know how far things have come for us, let me share the "What's Right With You Letter" I gave to Luke in 2003. At the end of the *31-Day Experience* you will write your kid such a letter.

Luke –

I have loved (and still do love) being your dad. I know that there have been times when I've been a good and wise father. And, I know that at other times I've angered you, frustrated you, been stupid, and generally messed up as a dad. Thank God for forgiveness and do-overs.

Anyway...I've been thinking recently about what's right with you. As I thought about this, I realized that I haven't told you in a while what is RIGHT with you from my perspective (besides the fact that you are good looking and just a stud in general).

So, here goes...my reminder of what's RIGHT with you.

First, you are a hard worker. You always have been and continue to be one. Very few people understand what it takes to do the work you do. Tireless hours, unexpected frustrations, unreasonable requests...and yet you work through it all. I admire how hard you work. You are an example to me. This inspires me.

Second, you have wonderful visual and aesthetic instincts. You did in high school as a lighting director, and you do today as a chef. You have an uncommon eye to see beauty and order. Trust these instincts; you have great intuition.

Third, you have a big heart. I know you blame me for this. This reality leaks out now and then...you know it does, you big softie! When mom got sick, you were the first one to the hospital sitting on the gurney next to her. You have no idea how much that meant to her. And recently when you were with grandma in her weakness and affliction, you expressed a strong and tender love to her. That was amazing. And when you're around kids with an opportunity to sincerely care for them...you light it up. As Logan would say, "That's tight dude!"

Fourth, you don't need much to be happy. This is an amazing thing considering we live in a world where people have to have so much stuff to survive—you are content. You have an innate ability to live on a little and embrace the simple and good things in life.

Fifth, you are a loyal, non-judgmental friend. You don't put down people who are struggling. You accept others where they are, and they feel that from you. I am your student as I watch this part of your life. Oh, and God help the person who trashes one of your friends. They just invited some serious trouble from you, a steadfast friend. I dig this about you.

Sixth, you have an ability to enjoy life. You smell the smells, taste the tastes, see the different shades of color, and recognize the beauty in small things. This is good and makes God smile because he loves it when we enjoy his gifts.

And seventh (and seven is the perfect number, you know), you are tough. Golly dang, you are one tough mother. Whether it has to do with enduring pain or putting up with difficulty, you are just plain tough.

Not bad...seven RIGHT things about Luke: hard worker, great aesthetic instincts, big heart, content, non-judgmental friend, enjoys life, and tough. I celebrate these about you, Luke...you should, too. Know I love and believe in you.

As always -- for you...anything, anytime, anywhere.

Dad

BEING SET UP FOR SUCCESS

The majority of kids today (especially teenagers) live with a low-grade fever of distrust toward adults. They feel that way for good reason. Many kids have been minimized, neglected, or left behind by adults who are absorbed with their own lives. Because of this, kids lean into each other and draw support from clusters of friends. Kids look at adults and feel that the only reason attention is paid to them is because adults want something from them. They want grades, performance, or someone they can brag about to their friends. Kids seriously wonder if anyone other than their friends care to get to know them. The truth is that most adults do not really want to take the time to understand and know them, let alone help them discover who they are.

I have discovered that when a kid deems you trustworthy and safe, he or she will often confide feelings of loneliness and abandonment by the adult community. Kids often only feel understood by their peers. It is interesting that even in the middle of multiple online social networks, kids still feel lonely and have deep wonderings about who they are and their futures. For this reason there will often be suspicion when you approach them to engage in this process of helping them discover who they are. So what do you do?

You will not be able to help kids discover who they are unless you are willing to be absorbed with their world. That is what compassion does: It looks away from itself and sees another. Jesus left heaven and fully engaged in our world to help us understand who we are and express the Father's love. That is our task, too, to leave our isolated little world and enter a kid's world to express God's heart while helping him or her discover a true sense of self. Your job is to step toward a kid and build a relationship that will allow for authentic discussion about who he or she is at the core.

"The majority of kids today (especially teenagers) live with a low-grade fever of distrust toward adults."

ASSESSMENT

"I have discovered that when a kid deems you trustworthy and safe, he or she will often confide feelings of loneliness and abandonment by the adult community."

PRE-WORK—THE RESENTMENT ASSESSMENT

Now it is your turn to assess. This means you have pre-work to do before you offer an invitation to this adventure of discovery. Whether you are engaging your own child or not, I encourage you to do a resentment assessment.

The resentment assessment determines the condition of your relationship with your kid. How is it right now? Is there any anger currently being expressed toward you? What is the source of it? Pay attention to anger beneath the surface. Resentment kills relationship. If there is anger, it will be difficult to engage in this process. Often times the best thing you can do is slow down and give him or her permission to relate true feelings, without judgment.

Ask your kid...

> ...how are we doing right now?

> ...how would you describe our relationship?

> ...are we far apart, kind of close, or close?

> ...have I done anything to hurt you recently?

> ...are you mad at me about anything?

> ...is there anything you need to say to me?

Then listen, apologize, talk it out, and move on. If he or she feels safe, true feelings will be revealed. Invite your kid to tell you when and how you have let him or her down. Do not judge or fight back. Work at understanding. Just listen and attempt to own your part of the breakdown. When you do this you are laying a foundation for future discussions.

It is easy to assume things are good between the two of you when they may not be. If you try to draw close and sense resistance, there is something there.

ASSESSMENT

I am amazed at how self-focused I can be at times. I can live in the land of wishful thinking month after month.

THE INVITATION

Once things are clean between the two of you, offer an invitation to engage in the *31-Day Experience.* You may want to write out what you want to say and read it to your kid. Maybe you feel OK about just looking him or her in the eye and making the invitation. You might want to make it official and have both of you sign a declaration of engagement and date it. That is not necessary, but here is a suggested invitation if you want to use one.

_____, I want to invite you to spend some time together discovering who you are. God has created you. God has invested talent, gifts, interests, and passions in you. These are all things that are right with you and make you unique. In a world that often tells you what's wrong with you and what you can't do, with God's help I want to help you discover what's right with you and what you can do.

God has designed life to be most joyful when we are touching the world at our place of talent, gifts, and interests. You are young and yet to discover the full array of these. I want to help you with this. If you are up for it, I would love for us to hang out and talk about the miracle that is you.

These conversations will focus on the positive, not the negative. Right now your life may feel like a mystery. As we talk together we will search for the clues that will help us solve the mystery of you. We are going to try to collect insights about who you are that will help guide you into your future.

There is so much darkness, pain, loneliness, and despair out there in the world. Together, with God's help, we will look for light, friendship, and hope. God has a future for you. The Bible says your future is a good one and full of hope. Jeremiah 29:11 says, *"For I know the plans I have for you," says the*

Lord. *"They are plans for good and not for disaster, to give you a future and a hope."* My desire is to help you find your good future with God's help.

If you'd be interested in doing this, I will help you. You will need to be honest and thoughtful in the process as we both look to God for help.

Date: _____

(my name) _____

(kid's name) _____

Once you have done the resentment assessment and offered the invitation, you are ready to go. Have a wonderful month as you launch fully into the KidUnique *31-Day Experience.*

As a review, on the following page, reread the behavior of the ACTIVE zone and purpose to live there as you help your kid discover who he or she is.

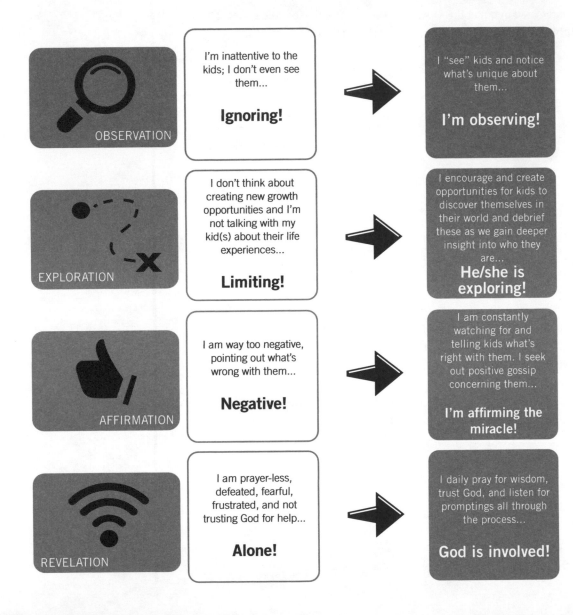

When I'm in the PASSIVE zone of relating to kids, the following is true of me...

Moving toward the ACTIVE zone = changing my mindset

When I'm in the ACTIVE zone of relating to kids, the following is true of me...

OBSERVATION

I'm inattentive to the kids; I don't even see them...

Ignoring!

I "see" kids and notice what's unique about them...

I'm observing!

EXPLORATION

I don't think about creating new growth opportunities and I'm not talking with my kid(s) about their life experiences...

Limiting!

I encourage and create opportunities for kids to discover themselves in their world and debrief these as we gain deeper insight into who they are...

He/she is exploring!

AFFIRMATION

I am way too negative, pointing out what's wrong with them...

Negative!

I am constantly watching for and telling kids what's right with them. I seek out positive gossip concerning them...

I'm affirming the miracle!

REVELATION

I am prayer-less, defeated, fearful, frustrated, and not trusting God for help...

Alone!

I daily pray for wisdom, trust God, and listen for promptings all through the process...

God is involved!

Endnotes:

1. John J. Ratey, *Spark: The Revolutionary New Science of Exercise and the Brain* (Little, Brown and Company, 2008), Chapter 1

2. Parker J. Palmer, *Let Your Life Speak: Listening for the Voice of Vocation* (Jossey-Bass, 1999), Chapter 2

3. Throughout this book I will be highlighting words and phrases that might need a little more explanation to understand. **"Sacred task"** is the first of many to come. A **"sacred task"** is an assignment given by someone or something greater than us. This is not just a good idea or a nice thought. I'm suggesting that this is an assignment given by God to one generation to invest in another.

4. **"Win in life"**...Winning in life for a kid is about discovering who he or she is and living joyfully and productively into their future. When kids feel good about who they are at their core they raise the probabilities that they will win in life.

5. **"Value"** is about worth. When a kid senses they (and those around them) have value, they treat the world differently.

6. For more information, see ***Hardwired to Connect***: www.americanvalues.org/html/hardwired.html

7. Chap Clark, *Hurt: Inside the World of Today's Teenagers* (Baker Book House, 2004). In this book, Chap Clark—professor of youth ministry and culture at Fuller Theological Seminary—talks about an eight-month break he took when he attempted to get to know the real condition of students in the public high school. He has taught about this age group and has been involved in student ministry for decades, but he wanted to get up close with kids and discover if they had changed in the last 30 years or so. To do this he spent eight months daily relating to kids at a public high school in Southern California. This bright veteran youth worker admits he thought he knew what was going on in the hearts of kids today. He shares how significantly his eyes were opened. So many discoveries were uncovered. But one that stunned him was the depth of hurt, abandonment, and loneliness felt by even the kids that had the most going for them. If your kid is a teenager you should read ***HURT*** so you can better understand his or her world.

8. "**Reflecting God's heart**" is a responsibility and honor. God's heart is so wonderful and relational, but many people miss that part—the relational part. Many people see God as just, righteous, and too lofty to attain. A theology of thinking you have to work to please God can cause you to lose your sense of a joy-filled relationship. God loves me. I love a kid because God loves my kid. Enough said!

9. "**Sort a kid out**"…identifying, clarifying, and investigating who he or she is, is all part of the sorting process.

10. "**Resistanc**e" is the force all around you and inside of you that wants to prevent you from entering and accomplishing this important task of helping a kid discover who he or she is.

11. Ken Robinson and Lou Aronica, *The Element: How Finding Your Passion Changes Everything* (Viking Press, 2009), Chapter 1

12. "**Like God**"…this doesn't mean we are God or playing God. But we are behaving like God behaves as he pays attention to things.

13. "**on the upside**"…the upside is the good side, the noble side, the side of a person you like and love. Think about a good friend…what is his or her upside? What comes to mind is what I mean here.

14. See Chapter 9 from **The REAL DEAL: Becoming More Authentic in Your Life and Leadership**. Available at authenticleadershipinc.com.

15. Luke is in his 30s at the time of this writing. He is in a great place today and we enjoy a close friendship. He has granted me permission to share some of our darker days in the hopes they will help others who are trying to find their way. He is married to Whitney, a wonderful woman, and currently enjoying a successful career as a chef in the food service industry.

31-Day Experience

Tony Schwartz and Chris Trethewey

Before you start the 31-Day Experience

Before you jump into the *31-Day Experience,* let me remind you of a few things...

Begin with the end in mind. The desired end is a closer relationship with your kid and significant discovery concerning who he or she is. Once you finish the month of exercises addressing the four-window model, your last assignment will be to create a *"What's Right With You"* letter that you will gift to your kid. Keep this in mind as you collect insights during the next month.

Know the age of your kid and make adjustments accordingly. Please do not let age keep you from going through this process. Whether your kid is 5 or 15, this experience can work for you. Take freedom adjusting the experiences to fit the age of your kid.

Be intentional. Go after this project like a child goes after chocolate chip cookies. The daily exercises are meant to take about 10 minutes, but the hope is that the thoughts they hold will trigger your imagination so that you reflect on these throughout the day.

Take your time. This is not about "RUSHING" through and getting this experience out of the way. Take your time. Give each day your best! Your kid deserves it. If you need to take a day and turn it into a week, go for it.

You will hit some walls. Count on this. Most likely you will not do every exercise. Some just may not fit right with your kid. That is fine. Do not let minor setbacks discourage you or prevent you from moving ahead. The benefits are just too important for your kid. If you miss an exercise, just move ahead to the next day's exercise. If you miss a couple days, no big deal. Just jump back in. If the *31-Day Experience* takes 60 days, that is fine. It is not about rushing; it is about relationship and discovery. Know that completing this will be worth it. It will bring you closer to your kid—count on it.

Be aware that there are only 20 actual daily exercises and that is on purpose. The *31-Day Experience* is broken into four weeks with an additional project that ties a bow on the month. Over the next four weeks you will have five daily exercises on each window. (Some of you may extend this experience to eight weeks and only do half the exercises each week.) After the five days of interacting with your kid, there is a day dedicated to wrestling with a list of Reflection Questions. These are there for you to answer with your spouse, small group, or alone. The seventh day of the week you will find a page titled *"Me In The Mix."* It will give you an opportunity to stop and think over the last week. Here is where you consider what you are learning about you. I believe this month will grow you as much as your kid, and it is important to track your learnings, not just what your kid is discovering.

Do the 31-Day Experience with someone. As mentioned above, one day a week is set aside for Reflection Questions. You will learn far more, and raise the probabilities of finishing, if you do this with a friend, spouse, or small group. Do not do it alone.

If you have more than one kid. In the daily exercises each "Active Zone" is designed for one kid. Feel free to make a copy of the active zone if you have more than one kid. Or just grab a piece of paper and do the Active Zone for each kid you have. You might consider doing this experience with just one kid at a time, beginning with your oldest. Then in six months do it with the next and so on. If you are going to do a couple kids at once get a notebook or journal to track your insights. Feel free to tweak each Active Zone to fit you and your kid. Everyone is different. We desire for you to make the most of each one. But (here is the big "but" clause), do not change it because it makes you feel uncomfortable. Face it, enjoy the journey, and experience the journey with your kid.

Do this again in a year or two with your kid. A year from now (or 10 years from now) you can repeat this entire experience and have a new and deeper layer of understanding. It will be fun to compare your experience now, in two years, or in 10-year intervals.

Have fun. Work hard. Pray daily. Believe God will help. And be seriously ridiculous with how you love your kid this month.

The 31-Day Experience
Week One: OBSERVATION

Day 1• You Know the Answers
Big Idea: "See" your kid today.

Day 2• Build Your Team
Big Idea: See your kid through the eyes of other people who love him or her.

Day 3• Time Test
Big Idea: Distractions in your life can hinder your ability to "see" your kid.

Day 4• Top 5
Big Idea: Discovering your kid's greatness together.

Day 5• Invisible Forces
Big Idea: You prove your love for your kid by understanding what makes him or her thrive...what pulls him or her.

Day 6• Reflection Questions used for personal or group study.

Day 7• "Me In The Mix"—a pause to consider what you are learning through this experience.

Week Two: EXPLORATION

Day 1 • Try It...You Might Like It
Big Idea: **Create opportunities for your kid.**

Day 2 • The Debrief
Big Idea: **Helping your kid sort out the experiences of his or her life.**

Day 3 • The List
Big Idea: **Learning more about your kid by identifying interests.**

Day 4 • The Interview
Big Idea: **Initiate a conversation with your kid.**

Day 5 • Connect
Big Idea: **Getting your kid around great people.**

Day 6 • Reflection Questions used for personal or group study.

Day 7 • "Me In The Mix"—a pause to consider what you are learning through this experience.

Week Three: AFFIRMATION

Day 1 • Feed the Heart (Part 1)
Big Idea: The three most powerful words you can speak to your kid.

Day 2 • Feed the Heart (Part 2)
Big Idea: The three most powerful phrases you can speak to our kid.

Day 3 • Positive Gossip
Big Idea: Passing on positive comments made by others about your kid.

Day 4 • On Record
Big Idea: Going on the record with your kid.

Day 5 • The Bottom Line
Big Idea: I need to speak these things to my kid.

Day 6 • Reflection Questions used for personal or group study.

Day 7 • "Me In The Mix"—a pause to consider what you are learning through this experience.

Week Four: REVELATION

Day 1 • God Speaks—the "GQ" (God Question)
  Big Idea: Inviting your kid into the process of listening to God.

Day 2 • Take a Walk and Listen (Part 1)
  Big Idea: Hearing heaven's thoughts about your kid.

Day 3 • Get Some Help
  Big Idea: Asking God for what you most want for your kid.

Day 4 • Real Influence
  Big Idea: Using God's Word to guide your prayers for your kid.

Day 5 • Take a Walk and Listen (Part 2)
  Big Idea: Hearing heaven's thoughts about you.

Day 6 • Reflection Questions used for personal or group study.

Day 7 • "Me In The Mix"—a pause to consider what you are learning through this experience.

Week Five: The Celebration

Day 1-6 • Creating your kid's "What's Right With You" letter

Day 7 • Presenting your kid with the "What's Right With You" letter

OBSERVATION – Day 1

"You Know The Answers"

Big Idea: *See your kid today.*

Go back and reread about the distractions that can keep us from seeing our kids.

(pages 35-41)

Distractions

• DRIBBLING WITH YOUR HEAD DOWN.

• ALLOWING THE MESS TO CLOUD THE MIRACLE.

• LETTING THE PREDICTABLE IRRITATIONS OF LIFE SABOTAGE YOUR RELATIONSHIP WITH YOUR KID.

Some things in life just take hard work, effort, and focus. Caring for a kid is one of those things. The crazy thing is that our kids do not come with a "how to" manual! We question ourselves as parents and those who care for kids sometimes, right? (nod: yes) We have all come to points in raising our kids where we feel semi-clueless and more than a little out of our league. Parenting and caring for kids is not easy!

Graduate school was not easy either. Check out this little story as your *31-Day Experience* begins....

I got through grad school with the help of a financial donor. The only catch was that I needed to ace every class. If I did not get an "A," I would not get reimbursed for the cost of the class. Needless to say, I really wanted to get the best grades possible. Parenting is a little like that. We want to do our very best, and we feel some pressure to make it happen.

Accounting classes were the toughest for me over the course of those four years. I still get weepy when I think about accounting terms and how hard that was for me. Before one critical exam that required a ton of memorization, I remember getting extra help before and after class time. Finally the day of the test came and I can still remember what my professor said to me as I walked into the lecture hall. He said, "Relax man, you know the answers."

Today, in the exercise that you are about to do, you know the answers. As you begin this *31-Day Experience*, let yourself relax.

MY ACTIVE ZONE:

"Those who leverage the Observation window understand that there is a story unfolding right before their eyes in the life of a kid they love and they slow down enough to 'see' it."
KidUnique, page 35

Slow down. Looking at the kid you love through the Observation window will come naturally. For some of us, it might take us awhile to get warmed up to this kind of focus. The key is to slow down long enough to actually do it. No one on the planet is as qualified as YOU to help your kid with the discovery process. So sit back, relax, and grab a pen.

Again, in the graph below, you will know the answers. Slow down and let it happen! Do not "edit" your thoughts as you write. Just answer the questions and let your words go where they go. Monitor your emotions as you think about your kid during the following exercise. Feel how blessed you are to have the treasure of your kid.

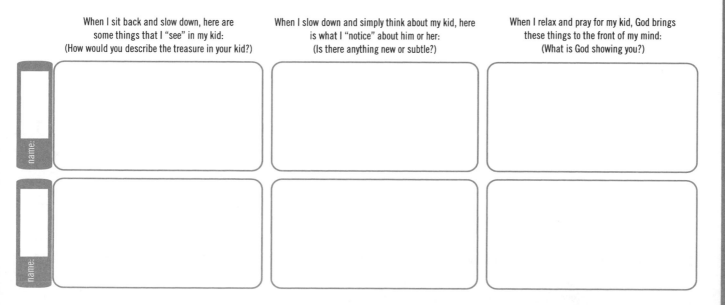

When I sit back and slow down, here are some things that I "see" in my kid: (How would you describe the treasure in your kid?)	When I slow down and simply think about my kid, here is what I "notice" about him or her: (Is there anything new or subtle?)	When I relax and pray for my kid, God brings these things to the front of my mind: (What is God showing you?)
name:		
name:		

Build Your Team

Big Idea: *See your kid through the eyes of other people who love him or her.*

Think of people who love your kid.
Jot down their names in the space below.

Include grandparents, family members, neighbors, friends, teachers, coaches...

Now, look at the list you just created. Think about this: Do any of those people have any meaningful input for you regarding your kid? Would any of the people you just listed have any significant observations of your kid? Do any of the people on your list have chances to see "the miracle side" of your child? The list above is your "team." This team might change a little over the years, but one thing will remain the same: These people care about your kid, and they care about you!

MY ACTIVE ZONE:

Since becoming a grandparent, my dad has been given the name "Poppy" by his grandkids. I just call him Pop. Not long ago, Pop got his boat fixed. We went out for a test ride to listen to the engine and make sure the boat ran well. As the engine hummed, we just sat together. I drove at different speeds to hear the engine under different stresses. The boat sounded smooth, so soon we just began to enjoy the ride and scenery. Poppy broke the quiet of our boat ride by saying this sentence:

"Those kids of yours sure are something."

There is a lot of love in a sentence like that. He is proud of his grandkids. My dad is on my team. Odds are good that you have heard a sentence like that spoken of your kid. Maybe it was one of their teachers or a neighbor friend. I noticed when my dad said that and I pushed him. I asked him to be more specific. "What do you mean?" I asked. He used some more general terms until I almost forced him to be specific. I asked about each one of my three kids by name. Here are the questions I used:

What do you "see" in them?

What are they good at?

When are they at their best?

Does anything concern you about them?

So, here is your observation exercise and action step for today. Seek out one of the people on your "team." Look back at the list you made and just pick one. Write an e-mail or make a phone call if you are not going to see him or her today. Explain your "KidUnique" mission and just ask what he or she "sees" in your kid. Use one or all of the questions above. Get some insight and tap into the brilliance of your team to help you observe your child.

Collecting these observations from your team is a fun thing! It gets even better when you communicate what they say about your kid to your kid! Use the next couple pages to record insights.

MY ACTIVE ZONE continued:

Before the day ends share with your kid a few of the insights you heard in your conversations with your friends. This will feed your kid's heart and be good practice for an exercise you will do later during the affirmation week.

My kid's name:

My friend's insight...

My kid's name:

My friend's insight...

MY ACTIVE ZONE continued:

Before the day ends share with your kid a few of the insights you heard in your conversations with your friends. This will feed your kid's heart and be good practice for an exercise you will do later during the affirmation week.

My kid's name:

My friend's insight...

My kid's name:

My friend's insight...

OBSERVATION – Day 3

Time Test

Big Idea: *Distractions in your life can hinder your ability to see your kid.*

Life. It is crazy. Hectic. Stressful. Overbooked. Full of distractions. Never ending. Pressure filled.

Sound familiar?

As I write this exercise, I am one week (well, 6 days, 7 hours and 23 minutes, but who is counting) away from a very much-needed vacation. I have several projects that I am trying to finish and a to-do list that is longer than my arm. This last week I have consumed enough caffeine (via venti black coffees) to energize a small island nation.

I am guessing that my life is not that much different from yours. Somehow in the middle of our busy lives we are to push aside distractions long enough to really "see" our kids. Fatigue and deadlines are currently blinding me to my kids and I do not like it. I wish technology would give me back time to observe my kids. It does not. Cell phones. E-mail accounts. Twitter®. Facebook®. Text messages. All these just create a communication traffic jam in my world.

There is a war being waged for our time. We are going to have to choose what gets our time and what does not, what gets our attention and what does not. We are going to have to decide whether or not we will declare war on the distractions so we can focus our attention on the kid we love.

Consider: What distractions most threaten the relationship you have with the kid you love? What most prevents you from being able to observe your kid? Is it competing time demands? Is it the strain of work? Is it having too many balls in the air? Do you have unresolved conflicts that rob your presence? Is there anxiety over finances? Are you mad about something? What is it? In today's exercise we have to get to the bottom of this and set a strategy for change.

Let us tackle this in today's exercise.

MY ACTIVE ZONE:

STEP #1: What things in your life are competing for your time with your kid? What things are distracting you from focusing on your kid? Write them down, no matter how big or how small.

STEP #2: Look over the list you just made and circle two distractions you can eliminate with careful planning.

STEP #3: What strategic steps do you need to take to get your priorities back in order? Write down two or three specific actions that will allow you to take control of your schedule and re-prioritize your time so that your kid gets quality and quantity time from you.

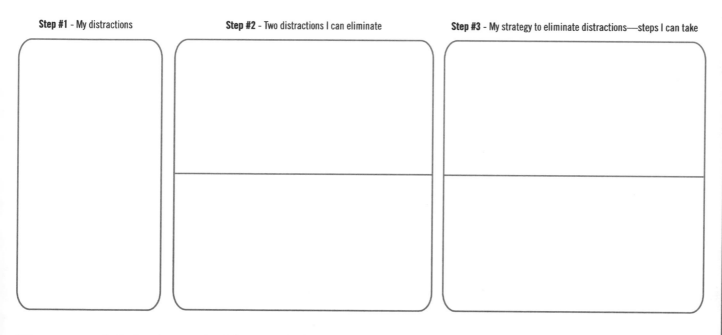

Step #1 - My distractions

Step #2 - Two distractions I can eliminate

Step #3 - My strategy to eliminate distractions—steps I can take

Who can you tell about your decision to eliminate these distractions? Give them a call right now and ask them to pray for you.

Who I am telling: _____   When I told them: _____

OBSERVATION – Day 4

Top 5

Big Idea: *Discovering your kid's greatness together.*

Michael Phelps is on the top of the sports world. Every country on the planet knows his name. He accomplished something that no one has ever accomplished and probably no one else ever will. He won 14 gold medals in the 2004 and 2008 Olympics, more than any other athlete, ever. He set a record at the 2008 Olympics, earning eight gold medals to surpass Mark Spitz's seven gold medals in the 1972 Munich Olympics. Phelps has a record-setting seven world-record times and earned the *Sports Illustrated Sportsman of the Year* in 2008. Truly this is an amazing feat of great accomplishment.

What many people do not know about Michael Phelps is that he did not have the easiest road to the success he accomplished in the pool. At a young age, his parents divorced and Michael would have very little contact with his dad after that. He was constantly made fun of at school for his big ears, weird body shape, and a lisp that would surround every word he spoke. At age 7, he was diagnosed with ADHD. His teachers were extremely hard on him because of his inability to focus and pay attention. Enter: swimming. This sport has allowed Michael to find his genius, his greatness. It gave him something to focus on and work toward. It was something that he could not only be successful at, but was successful at. He faced numerous obstacles, but with hard work, the help of a great coach, and the encouragement of his mom and sisters, Michael had the support he needed to become the best swimmer and the best Olympian in the world.

Every kid has incredible potential, genius, and greatness. Too often it is never discovered or put into play. Together, you and your kid can discover that greatness that resides inside. Read the exercise on the following page. You will come back and complete the chart below in a couple minutes.

Five Top Words That Describe My Kid

NUMBER 1	NUMBER 2	NUMBER 3	NUMBER 4	NUMBER 5

MY ACTIVE ZONE:

ambitious	detailed	flexible	kind-hearted	sensitive
brave	determined	friendly	likable	sincere
calm	diligent	funny	loving	smart
capable	dynamic	generous	obedient	talented
charming	eager	gentle	peacemaker	teachable
cheerful	encouraging	happy	productive	thoughtful
competitive	energetic	helpful	protective	thrifty
confident	entertaining	honest	punctual	tough
cooperative	enthusiastic	honorable	quiet	trustworthy
courageous	fair	impartial	reflective	unbiased
decisive	faithful	intense	responsible	wise

STEP #1: From the list above, identify five words that you think best describe your kid. Write them on the chart at the bottom of the previous page. For now, do not show them to your kid.

STEP #2: Have your kid look through the list above and on the chart CIRCLE the 5 words that he or she feels describe himself/herself the best. This might be a quick or slow process. Allow the time needed. If your child is young, you may need to read the list for them and explain or define some of the words. Feel free to add or delete words.

STEP #3: Have your kid share why each specific word was chosen. Do not argue with his or her choices. Listen, learn, and reinforce your kid's sincere efforts to do this task.

STEP #4: Now share your list with your kid. Share openly and honestly. This should be a great time to encourage and build up your kid.

Later consider:
1. What words did you both choose that were the same? What words are different?

2. Do you see your kid differently than your kid sees himself or herself? What did you learn about your kid by the words he or she chose?

OBSERVATION – Day 5

Invisible Forces

Big Idea: *You prove your love for your kid by understanding what makes him or her thrive.*

Remember Sir Isaac Newton? As the story goes, Mr. Newton was minding his own business, sitting under a tree one night and staring up into the sky. He was pondering how the universe functions, how gravity works, and gravity's impact on everything. He was thinking about the moon—how it orbits around the earth and how the inverse square law plays into this entire picture. You know, simple things. That night, as he lay there, an apple suddenly fell from the tree and (legend says) hit him on the head. That moment sparked a thought that took him on an unprecedented scientific journey. This journey changed what everyone had thought before and gave insights into the universe, opening doors that had never been opened before.

Science has proven that there are invisible forces at work all around us. Take your Uncle Sonny's old bowling ball and drop it on your big toe. You will feel the very real pain of the invisible force of gravity. Go eat a king-size bag of Taco Doritos® and swallow them down with a whole gallon of Mystic Mountain Blueberry Mountain Dew®. In approximately 17 minutes, you will definitely feel an "invisible force" in your body functions. Invisible forces in science are everywhere! Need more examples? No? Really?! Are you sure? OK.

None of us have ever seen gravity, but the pulling effect it gives is essential and influences everything we experience.

"What draws a kid is like a whisper in his or her head that we cannot hear."

KidUnique, page 46

MY ACTIVE ZONE:

As you observe your kid, you will also see "invisible forces" at work. Revisit the following excerpts from KidUnique and jot out some thoughts to the questions in the spaces provided. You might have written some notes in the margin as you read the Observation chapter—check back to read them, if you want.

> *"Let us think now on a deeper level about your kid. As I have already mentioned, kids behave the way they do for a reason. There are innate passions and interests living in your kid that will affect behavior and what he or she is drawn to. We must train ourselves to watch for what pulls at our kids. Read that last sentence again. The things kids truly love 'call' to them....what draws a kid is like a whisper in his or her head that we cannot hear. Deep interests pull at our kids. If they love art, the canvas calls. If they love music, the instrument calls. It they love math, numbers call. If they love dance, movement calls. If they love basketball, the gym calls."*
> KidUnique, page 46

What is "calling" to your kid? What "pulls" at your kid?
(try to be specific)

"There is a difference between things that kids are pushed into versus what they are drawn toward. We can push our kids into things that we think are cool but are a thousand miles from who they are. The 'pull factor' in a kid's life is far more important than the push factor. We want to discover what pulls them and encourage investigation."
KidUnique, page 46

Are you the "pushy" type? Do you have any regrets
in this area? (try to be specific)

"I have mentioned that most of us are quicker to see the downside of a kid than the upside. You may be able to identify in a moment three things that bug you to death, but it may really take some work to identify the upside. Before you interact with your kid, take the list of stuff that bugs you and commit it to God."
KidUnique, page 48

Take a moment and pray through the things that may bug you as you observe your kid. Be honest and get God's heart involved with yours.

"When you talk with your kid you will not have the whole picture, but you will have a small piece of the puzzle. Your relationship will be characterized by many of these brief 'glimmer' conversations. Keep your eyes open and watch. Celebrate who your kid is in each conversation."
KidUnique, page 50

What "glimmer" conversation can you have with your kid TODAY? Include details: What will you say and how will you say it?

OBSERVATION – Day 6

Reflection Questions

1. What has been the **biggest challenge** for you as you have attempted to "observe" your kid this past week?

2. What is **one positive thing** you have noticed in your kid this last week that you had not seen before?

3. What is **one painful observation** you have made concerning your kid this last week that will need to be a matter of continual prayer?

"There are invisible forces at work all around. You cannot see them, but you know they are there."

4. What are you learning about the positive **"pulls"** inside your kid?

5. How have you adjusted your schedule—reallocated your time, reorganized your priorities—so that your kid **gets your best**?

6. What is the **biggest shift** you need to make if you are to continue to consistently look through the Observation window?

OBSERVATION – Day 7

"Me in the Mix"

Big Idea: *What I am learning along the way.*

A phrase that best describes my experience with KidUnique this last week is...

Evaluate the five **OBSERVATION Window** exercises:

Check the ones you did: **Rate the Experiences:**

☐ **Day 1 - YOU KNOW THE ANSWERS**   So-so................pretty good................fantastic

☐ **Day 2 - BUILD YOUR TEAM**   So-so................pretty good................fantastic

☐ **Day 3 - TIME TEST**   So-so................pretty good................fantastic

☐ **Day 4 - TOP FIVE**   So-so................pretty good................fantastic

☐ **Day 5 - INVISIBLE FORCES**   So-so................pretty good................fantastic

Which exercise was best and why do you think it worked so well?

What has been happening in you this last week as you have interacted with your kid?

What have you noticed about your relationship with your kid?

Have you received any fresh thoughts from God?

Is there anything that needs changing in you so you can do better at KidUnique?

Is there an issue that has surfaced that you will need to think more about in the future?

PAUSE—Use the space below to record any other thoughts you want to keep track of as you move through the KidUnique experience.

EXPLORATION – Day 1

Try it...you might like it.

Big Idea: *Create opportunities for your kid.*

When I was a freshman in high school my parents gave me a Christmas gift that they thought would be a home run. I did not like it or want it. It was their "special" gift to me that year and I know they had thought a lot about it before giving it to me. As I rounded the corner to the Family Room, there it was. Sitting right at the base of the overly decorated Christmas tree—a guitar.

Today I look back and wonder why I was so upset. I stuffed it into the back of my closet and did not touch it for a year. My parents, wisely, did not react to my immaturity and allowed some time to pass. Then about a year later, I pulled the untouched instrument from the closet and stared at it. For some reason I was intrigued and drawn to it that day, whereas a year earlier I couldn't have cared less about the guitar. For some reason, now I wanted to learn how to play it. The lessons I took led to playing for my church worship team and then to the forming of a band with some friends. By my junior year in high school, guitar was my life. In college I discovered a passion and gift for leading worship.

Today I understand that my parents saw something in me that I did not see in myself at the time. They noticed a *pull* in me toward music that I was blind to. Because of their insight into me they sat down and did an exploration brain dump that led to the guitar gift. Today I look back and I am amazed at their love, generosity, and patience.

MY ACTIVE ZONE:

Your exercise today is to think about your kid and do a similar exploration brain dump. I want you to come up with some possible opportunities you can create for your kids that will let them explore more who they are. Come up with some ideas that will stretch your kids and get them out of their comfort zone. You want to learn something about them you currently do not know.

With that said, think back through last week's observations. What has caused your kid's eyes to light up? What created excitement? What has sparked interest? We've provided you with an Exploration dumping ground. Write down a bunch of Exploration activities that could be of interest to your kid that you can make happen. Use the four thoughts below as guardrails for your dumping ground activity.

GUARDRAILS - 1. Out of the box: Something your kid has never done before. **2. Uncomfortable:** Something your kid would be stretched (at least a little) doing. **3. Exciting:** Something that will spark an interest. **4. Extreme but possible:** Something that will have an element of fear or an element of going beyond the realm of comfort.

EXPLORATION DUMPING GROUND

Now What?

Look at your list. Does it make you yawn? If so, go back again and come up with better ideas. Then pick two from the list. Yes, only two. You can always come back later and finish two more. Now, commit to making this exploration activity happen. This is going to be a gift you give just like the guitar I received at Christmas. Write the activities in the boxes to the right and let your kid know what the plan is to make these a reality. When they participate in the activity watch, discuss, and learn about your kid. Remember..."*The Exploration window is about a kid exploring life and discovering himself or herself along the way.*"

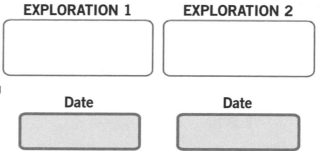

EXPLORATION 1

EXPLORATION 2

Date

Date

EXPLORATION – Day 2

The Debrief

Big Idea: *Helping your kid sort out the experiences of life.*

Does this sound familiar . . .

- Your kid comes home from the first day of freshman football practice and you ask: "How did it go?" The response..."All right." Frustrated by the lack of response, you either shut down or pop off with some crushing jab that slams the communication door air tight.

- Your kid flies in from a mission trip to a foreign country. You meet her at the airport. You give her a huge hug and quickly ask a bunch of questions beginning with, "How was it?" After the 10th "good," you stop asking questions, ending the short-lived conversation in awkward silence.

- Your kid completes the first day of junior high. Your stomach has been churning for over a week, and your prayers have consistently been focused on this issue. You drive to the school early to pick her up, and the anticipation of hearing about her day consumes you. She gets in the car, and your questions start to flow. You quickly wave the white flag and give up. Countless "OK" kill your enthusiasm to continue the discussion.

KidUnique adults will have these frustrating experiences. When they come we cannot stop engaging our kids. We must push forward and get better at entering conversation with them. We must develop the ability do to a "debrief." This is what today's exercise is all about.

MY ACTIVE ZONE:

The Debrief is a skill we must sharpen. Mike, a dad of four, discovered that the pathway to great conversation with his youngest boy was to sit down and play PlayStation® with him. While playing a competitive game of Madden®, he could ask almost any question and receive an honest response. My parents would simply ask me where I wanted to eat. I picked, they asked questions. I ate and answered freely. Every kid is different.

As your kid engages Exploration the important moments will need to be debriefed. Below are the elements of a successful Debrief. They are the **WHEN**, **WHERE**, and **HOW** of these discussions.

WHEN? Remember that your timing and your kid's timing might be different. Whenever possible change your timing to fit your kid's timing. Is your kid a morning person or does he or she wake up at 10 p.m.? Some kids tend to talk in the morning, some at night. Pick a time that works best for your kid.

WHERE? Location is important. Some kids chat in the car, some when in bed, and some at the dinner table. Pay attention to where they tend to open up. As you think about this be sure to give some space between you and your kid. My parents would often sit on the edge of my bed with the light out—it seemed to be safer to talk then. Have the conversation away from distractions. Turn off your cell phone! Turn off the television, radio, stereo, iPod—you get the idea!

HOW? Learn to ask open-ended questions: Stay away from "yes" and "no" questions. Ask follow-up questions, too. Simple questions will get your kid talking. *Example...What does _____ mean? How did that make you feel?* Most importantly, listen to what he or she is saying. Listen also for what is not being said. Listen to tone of voice. Say as little as possible. This is a time for them to share their experiences. Don't correct, make light, or reject their thoughts. If there is a need to provide challenge or push back, do so later unless your kid asks for your opinion right then. Look into his or her eyes.

Experiencing a Debrief...

Pick an experience your kid has had recently. Which one will you debrief?

When will you have the Debrief?

Where will you initiate the discussion?

How will you engage them...what are your first three questions?

What did you learn?

EXPLORATION – Day 3

The List

Big Idea: *Learning more about your kid by identifying interests.*

My dad and I have a great relationship, even though in many ways, we are exact opposites. He played basketball. *I played soccer.* He was class president. *I occasionally showed up to class.* He has little musical talent. *I rock with the best of them.* He was an amateur boxer. *I run like a little girl from trouble.*

I am grateful that my dad never tried to fashion me into his image. Over the years both he and my mom created space for me to explore and then asked me my thoughts, my desire, my passions. I was able to go fishing, hunting, and explored amazing parts of the country. I had chances to learn how to play piano and guitar, sing, and multiple other music-oriented opportunities. I was given a skateboard for Christmas one year, which quickly landed in the "not for me" pile. My dad put in a basketball hoop in the backyard; it was used more by birds than me.

The list goes on and on, but here is the point. *They created space for me to explore and then asked me my thoughts, my desires, my passions. They were intentional in picking out areas for me to explore that created excitement within me.* They also allowed me to move past areas that just were not me. Yes, they taught me the value of commitment and sticking through to the end, but there was always a finish line where they allowed me to walk away from something and explore something new.

What I remember most is that they explored with me. They did not dictate and dominate the ideas. They asked me and genuinely desired for me to pick areas that interested me. There were times when they picked for me (out of things they had observed). Sometimes they got it right and sometimes they did not. Being correct is not the goal; exploring is.

MY ACTIVE ZONE:

Today's exercise is for you and your kid to develop an "Exploration List." In the first Exploration exercise you created some ideas and made an experience happen for your kid. Today you create a list together. This should be a fun time for the two of you to dream together of all the different things he or she would like to do. Resist putting conditions and constraints on this list. Just writing something down here does not mean they will be able to do it. Maybe these will happen, maybe they will not. As you record ideas remind yourself that what they want to put on the list is a "tell" about them. Just keep that in mind and ponder later what these might be telling you about your kid.

Schedule a time to brainstorm areas to explore. These can be individual areas or as a family. This is a time to dream. It is OK if some ideas are outside the budget. Write them down anyway. Keep this list growing and developing. After your kid does one of the things on the list, debrief it together and learn.

Once the list is done, star a few that can be done this year. It does not matter exactly how many you pick; just make sure you can accomplish them. Your kid is counting on you to follow your commitment.

THE LIST
Exploration Ideas   **Date Experienced**

_____   _____

_____   _____

_____   _____

_____   _____

_____   _____

_____   _____

_____   _____

_____   _____

_____   _____

_____   _____

_____   _____

_____   _____

EXPLORATION – Day 4

The Interview

Big Idea: *Initiate a conversation with your kid.*

While I was driving Kiara (my 7-year-old) home from school the other day she said, "Dad, I want to be a dentist and a schoolteacher when I grow up." My wise thoughtful response was, "Oh, really." She proceeded to explain her reasoning for wanting to do both and ended her confident dissertation outlining the next 55 years of her life by telling me that as a dentist, "I am going to give every kid a sucker when they leave." Lovely.

Really, write something in the boxes!

When you were 7, what did you want to be?

What are you doing now?

Eighty percent of all incoming college freshman do not know what they want to major in. Once a major is chosen, 50 percent of college students will change their majors at least once. I know I changed my major several times. I am thankful for the role my parents and wife have played over the years as I sort out my life journey. They have allowed me to think out loud. They know when I am being dishonest or inconsistent with how I am at the core. Having great people help navigate each significant life step is powerful.

KidUnique adults have a powerful voice in a kid's life journey. Engaging your kid in meaningful conversations that touch his or her life is highly influential. It can guide and shape your kid's future. Meaningful conversation is not always easy to have with a kid. Depending on age and personality, you might have great interaction or just a get a blank stare. Do not focus solely on response. Taking the time to engage on a deep level will make an impact that will last a lifetime. I do not remember 97.34 percent* of all my conversations with my parents (*not a scientific poll). What do I remember is the overwhelming feeling that my parents were always there to help guide me and speak into my life.

The longing of a KidUnique adult is to move beyond only having five-minute conversations—those that happen as you flip through your e-mail, cook dinner, or play fetch with the dog. I am talking about the focused, one-on-one, intentional, no-time-constraints types of conversations when you engage your kid on a deep emotional level. When you step toward your kid and initiate conversation, your actions are speaking loudly. They are saying you care. Remember that it is always our actions that speak loudest.

Top Jobs from Kids
1. Astronaut
2. Athlete
3. Dancer
4. Doctor
5. Firefighter
6. Lawyer
7. Movie Star
8. Police Officer
9. Rock Star
10. Writer

MY ACTIVE ZONE:

Your exercise today is to schedule an "interview" with your kid. In this conversation you will ask a series of interesting and probing questions and then you will listen. You get to play Barbara Walters, and they get to be one of the most interesting people of the decade. Depending on the age of your kid, as well as personality and maturity, this conversation will have many different "looks" and outcomes. It is critical for you to capture your kid's uniqueness and form the interview around that. If you do not, success will be hindered. You may want to go back and review the skills of the Debrief from Exploration Day 2. These will frame your thinking as you approach your interview.

Preparing for the interview:

Location: where will it happen? _____

Choose a location that puts your kid at ease...where her or she will feel comfortable. You might throw out two or three suggestions and let your kid choose.

Timing: when will it happen?

Questions: create a list of questions to use on the next page.

Here are some questions to get you started:

1. What was the best moment of this last week?
2. When was the last time you laughed really hard?
3. When was the last time you felt fully alive? Really enjoyed life?
4. If you had a free day, what would you love to do?
5. What is one thing you hate doing?
6. Who do you really respect? Why?
7. What do you dream about?
8. What makes you nervous?
9. If you could be one thing when you grow up, what would it be?

"It is critical for you to capture your kid's uniqueness and form the interview around that."

kid's name

MY QUESTIONS

MY KID'S RESPONSES

WHAT I LEARNED ABOUT MY KID:

EXPLORATION – Day 5

Connect

Big Idea: *Getting your kid around great people.*

Every Friday morning throughout my junior and senior years in high school, my dad and I would leave the house early, grab breakfast, and talk life. It was one of those Father/Son, no-pressure times when he and I would just connect. Sometimes we had deep, life-changing conversations. Other times, we just talked about surface issues. The "what" was not as important as having time to connect one-on-one. Many of these mornings my dad only saw the top of my head as I laid it on the booth table top. But he never quit meeting with me and trying to make our times together special. He was patient and persistent. We met regularly—I could count on it even when I did not think I wanted to.

On one of those mornings my dad asked me if I had ever considered working for State Farm® Insurance, a company he had worked at since he left the military. I had actually thought about it. But I was not sure what I would do for State Farm®. The idea of a corporate job did intrigue me.

That day my dad booked a meeting for me with a bigwig at State Farm®. He wanted to expose me to a great person with the hopes that I might get some clues as to my future vocation. I felt nervous and excited as the day approached. My dad prepped me for the meeting. He had me create questions to ask and coached me on how to ask a follow-up question. He discussed proper dress code and how to handle myself. He laid out simple people interaction techniques (like looking someone in the eyes) that I would probably have forgotten because of the pressure of the meeting. Looking back, he was preparing me for every future interview. (Thanks, Dad!)

The day of the meeting came. I walked in, looked the man in the eyes, and gave a firm handshake. Then I began by asking my first question. The hour he had scheduled flew by in a flash. I thanked him for his time, walked out of the office, and headed straight to my dad's office. My mind was spinning with thoughts and questions about my future direction. That confusion was not a bad thing. It just raised more questions and the opportunity for a wonderful debrief with dad. Because I was exposed to a great person I was able to broaden my vision of what could be.

MY ACTIVE ZONE:

Today's exercise is to set up a meeting between someone great and your kid. The someone great may be a person who has specific expertise and experience in an area of interest to your kid. Maybe it will be a coach, artist, assemblyman, mayor, professor, business professional, or pastor. Your kid gets to do some exploring in this meeting. Be sure to tell your kid why this is a great person for them to meet.

What is an area your kid has an interest to explore? _____

Who is someone with expertise you can expose them to? _____

MEETING PREP: Help your kid succeed by giving him or her a little coaching.

> **1. LOCATION:** Who the meeting is with and what it is about will determine the "where." For me, the corporate office was a great location. Dinner at your house is another great possibility. It is more laid-back and relational. Be intentional with the location.

> **2. QUESTIONS:** Help your kid come up with a list of questions to ask. You might have him or her work on this alone first to encourage thinking through the process. Then you can sit and talk through the questions, and together brainstorm additional questions to ask.

> **3. PERSONAL CONDUCT:** Your goal is to prepare your kid to succeed at this. This type of interaction can be overwhelming for anyone at any age. Here are some guiding .thoughts: Firm handshake; Eye contact; How to begin the conversation; Follow-up questions; How to end the conversation; Saying thanks—a verbal thank you and a handwritten note.

THE DEBRIEF

After the meeting, set up a debrief with your kid. This is critical for the experience to take root. You can help talk through everything discussed to find out what excites and motivates your kid. If this is something your kid wants to explore more, set up another meeting with someone else. If it is something that your kid does not want to explore further, turn your attention to another great person. It is just important to get our kids around people who do vocational jobs that they might someday choose. Expose your kids to lots of great people and see who they connect with. This will give you one more clue into who they are.

EXPLORATION – Day 6

Reflection Questions

1. What have you learned about your kid as you have attempted to inspire him or her to explore, and paid attention to their reactions?

2. Did you make any discoveries about yourself as you attempted the "debrief" exercise? What were they?

3. What is one insight you have had concerning your kid that you have no idea what it means and you find yourself saying "I'm not sure, it's too early to tell"?

"When we are looking through the Exploration window we are learning to use opportunities to discover insights about our kids."

4. Have you been surprised by any of your kid's **reactions** to exploring and debriefing this week?

5. What have you learned about how **imaginative** and **flexible** you are when it comes to exploring?

6. What is the **biggest shift** you need to make if you are to continue to consistently look through the Exploration window?

EXPLORATION – Day 7

"Me in the Mix"

Big Idea: *What I am learning along the way.*

A phrase that best describes my experience with KidUnique this last week is...

Evaluate the five **EXPLORATION Window** exercises:

Check the ones you did:	**Rate the Experiences:**
❑ **Day 1 -** TRY IT, YOU'LL LIKE IT	So-so................pretty good................fantastic
❑ **Day 2 -** THE DEBRIEF	So-so................pretty good................fantastic
❑ **Day 3 -** THE LIST	So-so................pretty good................fantastic
❑ **Day 4 -** THE INTERVIEW	So-so................pretty good................fantastic
❑ **Day 5 -** CONNECT	So-so................pretty good................fantastic

Which exercise was best and why do you think it worked so well?

What has been happening in you this last week as you have interacted with your kid?

What have you noticed about your relationship with your kid?

Have you received any fresh thoughts from God?

Is there anything that needs changing in you so you can do better at KidUnique?

Is there an issue that has surfaced that you will need to think more about in the future?

PAUSE—Use the space below to record any other thoughts you want to keep track of as you move through the KidUnique experience.

AFFIRMATION – Day 1

Feed the Heart – Part 1

Big Idea: *The three most powerful words you can speak to your kid.*

Right around the first Monday of every month during college, I would get a check in the mail. The check was for $120 (my spending money for that month) and there would be a note attached. The money came from my mom and dad and the note would be a simple one- or two-sentence encouragement of some kind.

Pretty cush for a college kid, right? Not a big deal, you might say. It was not a ton of money, but it gave me gas money so I could continue to serve where God had called me to, in student ministry. Beyond the money, it was significant to me for one reason: the little note was always in my dad's handwriting. I cherished those little notes simply because I could read *"Love, Dad."* My dad rarely tossed out the verbal "I love you" affirmations to us kids. Dad showed his love for us, but he didn't say the words a whole lot. He showed it big-time through his presence in our lives and the way he provided for us. I know he loved me, but growing up, he said those three words to me only a handful of times. My mom, on the other hand, was all over the "I love you" deal—I heard it several times a day from her. For whatever reasons, guys like my dad, from his generation, did not often say those words.

Think back: Can you remember how it felt to hear "I love you" from your mom and dad? Can you still hear their voices in your head? Some of us had parents like my mom who said it all the time. Some of us do not remember hearing "I love you" much growing up. Whatever your experience was, we can all agree that expressing this specific affirmation to our kids is significant. Do not underestimate how much your kids need to hear, feel, and know that you love them!

"The Affirmation window turns loose a potentially transforming power. It has the potential to unleash a kid's gifts upon the world and unlocks the God-given extraordinary."

MY ACTIVE ZONE:

In the next 24 hours, you have a checklist to complete. The list contains three jobs. Check the boxes when you are done with each job. Easy!***

☐ ### Job #1 – Say the Words

Today, at least once, say the words "I love you" to your kid. Not the lame "I love you" as he or she goes out the door to school—anybody can do that. You are KidUnique, and we expect more from you! Make some eye contact happen and say it! Make sure your kid feels it. *(Note: If you have teenagers, they might pretend to be "too cool" for this. That's OK. Most teenagers suffer from temporary age-related brain damage. DON'T SHRINK BACK from saying the words!)*

☐ ### Job #2 – Touch

Today, at least once, express "I love you" to your kid through your touch. It might be a hug good night where you squeeze a little longer. It might be a little back rub as you talk. It might be your arm around him or her as you tell a story. One dad I know has begun the habit of holding hands with his 5 year old daughter when they are driving somewhere. Whatever it is, communicate "I love you" with some physical contact.

☐ ### Job #3 – Focused Attention

Today, at least once, communicate value to your kid with your attention. Focus your attention on your kid for a period of time. Make eye contact. Lean in and listen—be completely present. No TV. No iPhone. No laptop e-mail. No newspaper. No multi-tasking. If your kid is little, get down on the floor and "play" with him or her. Communicating this kind of value is a way to say "I love you" because you are proving that your kid matters enough to give your full attention.

*****OK, this might not be "easy" for you. In fact, it might be really difficult! You might be shy. You might have some walls up with your kids. You might have "stuff" in your life that gets in the way. Do not beat yourself up if you can not check one or more of these boxes right now. Lean into God's grace and let him set you on a path to bust the walls down.*

AFFIRMATION – Day 2

Feed the Heart – Part 2

Big Idea: *The three most powerful phrases you can speak to your kid.*

One of my kids, Robby, has moderate to severe hearing loss. Because of that, he wears hearing aids. Robby loves those hearing aids! Without that technology, he would have real trouble functioning at school, with friends, and in sports. When he climbs into bed to go to sleep, he will say "good night" and place his hearing aids on the dresser next to his bed. When those aids are out of his ears, he cannot hear much of anything. One of my favorite times with Robby is when I lean down to his little ears when he is not wearing his aids. I will speak clearly and directly right into his ears. I will not say much, usually just a phrase. He loves it and so do I. He has the blanket pulled up and his eyes closed and he just smiles when I talk into his ear. Last night, here's what I said:

> ## *"You've got a huge heart, buddy.*
> ## *Dad's so proud of you."*

You have moments like that. Moments when you say powerful words—and your kid hears you. Really hears you. Listen, when you lean into your kid and speak powerful words—it matters! Let your kids hear these phrases from you:

> *"I'm proud of you."*
>
> *"You are very gifted."*
>
> *"Your future is so bright."*

MY ACTIVE ZONE:

Take a look at this quote from KidUnique.

> *"Affirmation is telling your kid what is right with him or her...it is noticing, and then communicating verbally, the upside truth of who he or she is and the talents God has provided."*
> KidUnique, page 71

This next exercise is going to make you smile...

Use the next few minutes just "noticing" your kid. Use the questions below to simply be thoughtful about your kid. Do not write a novel; just jot down some unedited comments about your kid in relation to the questions in each box. Have fun with this and be open to God's voice as you write...

What are the "specifics" that make me proud of my child?

Some examples to spur your thinking...

- "I can't get over how kind he is."

- "She cares about hurting people."

- "She loves God!'

- "He inspires me with his honesty."

Now make your list:

-

-

-

-

How is my kid uniquely gifted?

Some examples to spur your thinking…   ***Now make your list:***

- "My kid is SO creative…."   •

- "He can burp on command."   •

- "She can run wicked fast!"   •

- "My kid is smart."   •

Why does my kid have a bright future?

Some examples to spur your thinking…   ***Now make your list:***

- "My kid has no 'quit' in him."   •

- "People love being around her."   •

- "He truly cares about doing right things."   •

- "She can burp on command."   •

Next Step

SAY IT! Use the three phrases and be specific! Your kids will hear you and they want to hear you. Look for opportunities to speak these truths into your kid! These are phrases that you can say in the "cracks" of your family life. It doesn't have to be something carefully planned out (although it can be)—just be alert and deliver the goods! Don't hold back, and be clear.

Check this out:

*"Affirmation is not blowing sunshine at a kid. It is not lying or just blabbing fluffy happy thoughts….
It is trying to see into a kid and point out who he or she is, what gifts God has given and the person he
or she can become."*
KidUnique, page 76

AFFIRMATION – Day 3

Positive Gossip

Big Idea: *Passing on positive comments made by others about your kid.*

Scenario 1:

Mom buckles her preschool daughter into her car seat after a grocery store run.

Mom: Ellie, I forgot to tell you what our babysitter Amber said about you last night when we got home.

Ellie: What did Amber say, Mom?

Mom: She told me that she loves getting to spend time with you! She said you are kind and nice to her and that playing with you is really special.

Ellie looks out the window and smiles in the back seat...

Scenario 2:

Dad cracks open his 17-year-old's door just before 10 p.m.

Dad: Hey bud, you need to hear this—got a second?

Logan: What's up? *(he pushes away from a desk full of homework...)*

Dad: You know how we've talked about your coach's "colorful" language and how I don't really like his swearing?

Logan: Yep. Uh oh, what did he say now?

Dad: He pulled me aside tonight after your game and he told me something interesting about you. He said that you're the best "blankety blank" soccer player he's seen this year and the best goalie that he's ever coached! Can you believe he said that?!

Logan: Really? He said that?! What did you say back to him?

Dad: I just smiled, bud. And then I agreed with him. Way to go, man...

As the dad leaves the room, Logan sits back and smiles...

Scenario 3:

Mom is having a long-distance phone conversation with Grandpop.

Mom: G-Pop, would you mind writing Robby and Riley a note about what you just told me? Mainly, that you're so glad that their hearts are so big for God.

Grandpop: You mean about how proud I am of them? Why sure! That's a great idea...I'll write it just like I told you.

Mom: Add details, Dad. Those guys will love to read that kind of letter! That's something they will treasure up the road.

Grandpop: Consider it done!

Mom imagines a note like that written in her dad's cursive handwriting...she smiles.

MY ACTIVE ZONE:

One of your jobs is to chase down positive gossip about your kid. You are not alone in your task of helping a kid discover who he or she is. Teachers, coaches, family members, youth pastors, and others know and care about your kid. Ask these people for insight into the positive things they see.

Today is all about getting active in chasing down positive gossip about your child. Follow these **three steps** and allow this concept of "positive gossip" to take root in your relationship with your kid.

Step 1 – Get Help and Pray Specifically

Pray that God would supply you with an ongoing stream of positive gossip that will build up your kid. Specifically, ask God to give you positive gossip sources to help your kid answer these two questions:

1. "Am I lovable?"

2. "Do I have what it takes to be successful?"

Step 2 – Find the Sources

Who in your life has some "positive gossip" about the kid you love?

Go back to page 80 in KidUnique and transfer the names you wrote down there into the graph below along with what they said about your kid. If you need to make a phone call or two or send an e-mail to some of these people to get their feedback, do it. Simply ask them for what you need: *Positive Gossip.* Think through family members, teachers, friends' parents, neighbors, coaches, bosses...don't hurry this!

Positive gossip source #1 _____

What was said: _____

Positive gossip source #2 _____

What was said: _____

Positive gossip source #3 _____

What was said: _____

Positive gossip source #4 _____

What was said: _____

Step 3 – Attack!

Start passing it on! Think about how you are going to pass on the positive gossip that you are accumulating. START TODAY. The scenarios on pages 157-158 might help you to visualize how this is going to work. Timing is important. Say these things at times when your kid has "space" to hear the affirmation and digest it. Pay attention to Scenario 3. Some of the positive gossip that you hear might be best communicated by the people saying it! Can you get them to call your kid or write a note?

AFFIRMATION – Day 4

On Record

Big Idea: *Going on the record with your kid.*

Some words stick.

The writer of the story you are about to read is a guy named Bruce. He is a high school teacher in Montana who has a heart to help families. Check this out:

> When I was 13, in eighth grade, we got one of those stock letters sent from the school: "Your son/daughter has achieved honor roll for the third quarter." You know the type. This was not unusual for me or my sisters as we were all, for the most part, A and B types of students. In fact, this was just expected of us.
>
> So at some point, shortly after that letter arrived, I did some knucklehead thing that 13-year-olds do. I do not remember what it was; left the garage door open, left a hose running, failed to put my bike away, take your pick. Thirteen-year-olds do this stuff. My father's reaction, though, was generally not very patient or graceful in these situations, and in this one in particular it was especially capricious. He had a heart of gold but the temperament of a badger. What he said was, "Sometimes I wonder whether or not you're a little retarded." He did not laugh; it was not a joke or a jibe. He said it with an angry edge that implied seriousness. I have never tried to describe the feeling it brought on. It was not the "hammer blow"' or the "knife to the heart" that usually accompanies such terrible statements. It felt like I disintegrated inside. It came out of nowhere. I was completely vulnerable to the authority of my father's words, and they came without precedent or warning. It was as if my spirit melted and there was nothing left inside.
>
> I do not remember showing much emotion at the moment, not in front of him. What I did do, and do with deliberate purpose, was find that recent stock letter that said I was smart and did a good job in school and tore it in half.

"When you affirm a kid... you are saying, 'Yes, you have what it takes! Every right thing about you that I identify and pass on will remind you of that. Believe these things and live into them.'"

I must have left it in the open because that same evening, Mom confronted me with it. With real sadness, she wanted to know why I had done that. My explanation was that either Dad was right or that letter was right. I was having a hard time, in the moment, believing a letter over my own father. It was visceral.

Well, here's the upshot of the story. I still have that letter from the school. It is stained from the tape my mom put it back together with that has long since dried up and cracked away. It resides in a decorative folder tucked behind my high school diploma, which is displayed with my other diplomas in the classroom where I teach. It is a reminder to me of the power of words and the damage that can be done by loving and complicated authority figures. I do not want my dad to be the bad guy in this. There was more to him than this incident. In fact, upon his death there were, and continue to be, much more good things than bad. That said, this episode in my life will stick with me...

MY ACTIVE ZONE:

Bruce's story is striking. Words really do stick with us, especially the words spoken to us by parents, both the positive words and the hurtful ones. Chances are good that all of us have both kinds of memories from childhood. Why? Because some words stick.

Today's exercise centers on making our words stick with our kids by going "on record." The skill we are building today in the Affirmation window is to write notes to our kids. When something is "on record," it is saved and preserved. It is tangible and real. Building this skill is how we can go "on record" with our affirmation. Choose one (or more) of the options on the next page and get it done TODAY.

Before you get started, go back and read the "why" and the "what" behind what you're going to write. Go back and reread pages 77-79 and remind yourself what writing out your affirmation can mean to your kids and the rest of your world.

Going "On Record" - Writing Notes of Affirmation to Your Kids

Option #1 – Drop It Off at School

Write a quick affirmation note to your kid. Take it to the school and go to the office and explain to the school secretary what you're up to. Have the note delivered to your kid sometime during the school day.

How special do you think your kid will feel?

Option #2 – Hidden Notes

Write a quick affirmation note (or notes) and hide them in some places where your kid will find them soon: Backpack. Toy box. Under the pillow. Attached to a key ring. Wherever.

Do you think this will make his or her day?

Option #3 – Text It

If you do not text very much on your phone, now's your chance. Punch your thoughts into your keyboard and hit "send." Do it once, or text your kid all day!

Will your kid love this?

Option #4 – Be Obnoxious

Yeah, you can do this. Go "on record" in a big and public way. Write your affirmation on your kid's car windows. Write it on the bathroom mirror. Buy a banner and hang it in your subdivision (yowza). Decorate his or her locker. Do not be lame and embarrass your kid, but think about your words and do something fun. Get creative with this and enjoy the opportunity to encourage your kid!

Will this knock your kid over or what!?

DO IT NOW!

That's right...DO IT NOW!

The Bottom Line

Big Idea: *I need to speak these things to my kid.*

When children are very young (and parents very inexperienced), we focus on the specifics of parenting. With a newborn, parents are concerned about EVERYTHING: what he or she ate, how much of it was eaten, and whether it was healthy food. Parents even count how many poops a kid has in a day! As kids get older, parents get consumed with individual homework assignments, sports teams, friend selection, social skills development, church involvement, and getting along with one another. All of these things are important and have their places. Parents want to do their best for their kid, so they pay close attention! It's incredibly complex.

This is a very normal experience for parents in our culture. Parents in our culture also ask a very common question…

"Does anyone else ever think that parenting

is so complex that it's easy to get lost

in things that do not really matter?"

MY ACTIVE ZONE:

Today, let us get away from the complex and focus on "the bottom line." Take a few minutes and laser in on the basic messages or truths that you want your kid to know. Think about those messages in relation to this quote from KidUnique, page 72:

"Why is it that our kids seem to be infected with a low-grade fever of insecurity and inferiority? It is because they live in a world of comparison and often only see who they aren't instead of who they are. This is incredibly toxic to self-esteem."

You love your kid more than anyone on Planet Earth. As you think about your kid uniquely, what affirmation or truths does he or she need to know are really true? Force yourself to narrow it down to the irreducible minimums. Be simple. Be specific to your kid's heart! Today is about "bottom line" truth specific to your kid.

Thoughtfully complete the exercise below. You can only choose the "top" three for your kid specifically. There are some possible words below the boxes, but feel free to use your own words.

[my kid's name] _____ needs to know these 3 truths from me.

• I am so glad that God blessed me with you. • I am for you. • I am so proud of you. • I trust you. • I love you like crazy. • I am pleased with you. • I believe in you. • I admire you. • I don't want to "fix" you. • I am inspired by you. • I have forgiven you. • I worry about you. • I am committed to you. • You make me smile. • You are awesome! • You are beautiful. • You are complete. • You have what it takes. • I have confidence in you. • I want to repair our relationship. • You are on my mind all the time. • I love you without conditions.

AFFIRMATION – Day 6

Reflection Questions

1. What has been the **biggest challenge** for you as you have attempted to "affirm" your kid this past week?

2. What have you learned about **your kid** as you engaged affirmation?

3. What have you learned about **yourself** as you engaged affirmation?

4. Which method of affirmation was **easiest** and which **most difficult** for you? Why is this true?

Say it?

Write it?

Positive gossip?

5. Which of the **two key questions** affirmation answers most touches your kid? Why do you think that is? What more can you do to answer these questions for your kid?

Am I lovable?

Do I have what it takes?

6. What is the **biggest shift** you need to make if you are to continue to consistently look through the Affirmation window?

AFFIRMATION – Day 7

"Me in the Mix"

Big Idea: *What I am learning along the way.*

A phrase that best describes my experience with KidUnique this last week is...

Evaluate the five **AFFIRMATION Window** exercises:

Check the ones you did:	Rate the Experiences:
☐ **Day 1** - FEED THE HEART PART 1	So-so...............pretty good...............fantastic
☐ **Day 2** - FEED THE HEART PART 2	So-so...............pretty good...............fantastic
☐ **Day 3** - POSITIVE GOSSIP	So-so...............pretty good...............fantastic
☐ **Day 4** - ON RECORD	So-so...............pretty good...............fantastic
☐ **Day 5** - THE BOTTOM LINE	So-so...............pretty good...............fantastic

Which exercise was best and why do you think it worked so well?

What has been happening in you this last week as you have interacted with your kid?

What have you noticed about your relationship with your kid?

Have you received any fresh thoughts from God?

Is there anything that needs changing in you so you can do better at KidUnique?

Is there an issue that has surfaced that you will need to think more about in the future?

PAUSE—Use the space below to record any other thoughts you want to keep track of as you move through the KidUnique experience.

REVELATION – Day 1

God Speaks—the 'GQ' (God question)

Big Idea: *Inviting your kid into the process of listening to God.*

Think back. It is pretty easy to remember the hurtful messages that you got as a kid, right? Remember the junior high boy who bullied you and called you names? Yep. Remember the times you felt inadequate or afraid growing up? Check. Pretty much all of us can relate to some degree. For some of us, there are more negative and truly painful "messages" in the past than we care to dig up.

OK, move with me to a different place in your memory. Can you reflect back on the times that God either got your attention or tried to make you notice something about yourself? The reality is, you might not have labeled any of these moments as God "speaking" to you. Maybe this is a foreign concept to you. If it is, you are not alone. That does not change the fact that God does speak. The Bible is clear about God's heart to communicate with (and through) his creation. Whether you have noticed it or not, God has been communicating with you nonstop since you became you! Think about it. Try to focus in and remember. This might be hard for you, but give it a try.

I gave this some thought today. Here are three times in my childhood when I remember God speaking into my life. Check these out. They might help jog your memory as you imagine these scenarios:

Age 8 – I was in a backyard sandbox with two neighbor kids. They were brothers, 5 and 6 years old. The older kid threw a handful of sand at the younger boy and it escalated to a sandbox brawl. I stepped in and broke up the mini-battle by holding them back from each other and reasoning with them. For a minute or two, I talked to the little guys about being kind to each other. Just then, I felt their mom's hand on my shoulder. Making eye contact with me, she said that she had been listening to what I told her boys and that I was a "remarkable boy." I can still remember riding my bike home thinking about that. I did not know what "remarkable" meant back then. I do now. God spoke to me through that experience.

Age 12 – I held my newborn niece Jenna the morning she was born. I can still remember seeing her five little fingers grip my thumb. God spoke to me that day. It was one of the first times that I remember being aware of God's presence. As I held that little girl, God said to me "I am here, too." I was in awe.

Age 17 – I was a part of a great football game that our team happened to win. We were not supposed to win. In fact, most people thought we would get demolished. I played the game of my life, better than I thought I could play. In the school parking lot after the game, I dumped my bag into the back of my car and slammed my trunk. I turned around and saw one of my coaches behind me in his car as he left to go home. He did not lower his window to say anything to me. He just stopped his car, looked at me, smiled, then he winked and drove away. As I drove the four miles to my house, I felt God say to me "you're good." It was a quiet affirmation. It was clear and distinct, and I will never forget God's voice on that Saturday afternoon.

> ## "God speaks to your kid,
> ## and he wants to be heard."

MY ACTIVE ZONE:

Here is the deal: God speaks to your kid, and he wants to be heard. In order for you to help direct your kid to hear God's voice, it is helpful for you to have some firsthand experience. Take some time to think back on your life and try to remember some of God's communication to you. Relax with this. Do not force it. It might be difficult, and that is OK. Look back over the story of Mike Singletary and his mom in the first few pages of Chapter Six. You have experiences like that...go back and find them. In the next few minutes, use the boxes below and jot out some thoughts of the times that God has spoken to you in your childhood and teen years.

"God's Voice to Me" - #1   my age:

"God's Voice to Me" - #2   my age:

"God's Voice to Me" - #3   my age:

Next Step: GQ

If your kid is in junior or senior high school, it might be time for you to ask "the God Question." Figure out the right time and place to have a conversation with your kid about this question: *Have you ever sensed God saying anything to you about you and your future?* You can get the ball rolling by telling some of your memories/stories (the ones that you just wrote down.) Use this time to teach your kid about the fact that God does speak, and prompt him or her to listen for him. Help your kids to listen for God. Chances are that your kid might not have a ready answer to this GQ—do not worry about that! You two having this conversation will open the path to the process of learning to listen for God's leading and voice in your kid's life.

How did the GQ conversation go? Record below the highlights (or lowlights).

REVELATION – Day 2

Take a Walk and Listen – Part 1
Big Idea: *Hearing heaven's thoughts about your kid.*

Noise. Our world is a noisy place. There are voices everywhere. TV is in the background. The furnace kicks on and off. Harleys. Sirens. Traffic. iPods. Sports radio. The noise in our lives gets a little crazy sometimes, doesn't it?

 How about your voice—do you ever get sick of the sound of your own voice? If you are a parent, you probably do. Remember your parents' voices? Guess what. Now you are the parent and your kid hears your voice in some of the same ways that you heard your parents. Some of that reality is good and some of it is scary! We talk to our kids a lot and that's not a bad thing. You don't want to nag your kids, but sometimes you do. You try to fight the temptation to constantly "fix" your kids, but you love them so much that it can be hard to control. We give instructions and we help with homework. We communicate our love and we try to issue warnings when needed. We are on the job! If your kids are little, you're in almost constant verbal contact 15 hours every day and then you have a monitor going through the night. If you have junior high or high school kids, you're checking in a few times during the day. Staying connected is a big deal.

We listen to our kids a lot, too. How cute is your little one as he or she talks about the day? Think about it. If you have a teenager, you listen to the different "drama" scenarios of school, friendships, sports, and dating stuff. In fact, most parents wish their teenage kids would talk MORE! Some of us feel spikes of guilt because our schedules limit our time to listen and just be with our kids. A sad reality is that some of us have walls up with our kids for whatever reasons, so the lines of communication aren't open at all. If that's your situation, it hurts, doesn't it? We are listeners—that is part of our role.

OK, are you ready for some more parental noise? How about the sound of your own voice in your head when you second-guess yourself? It sounds like a crazy semester of psychology, but the truth is that parents can get pretty neurotic! Here is some of the noise in our minds that gets us twitchy and worked-up:

- **"Am I being too protective?"**

- **"Do I push too hard?"**

- **"Am I out of touch?"**

- **"I'm a control freak!"**

- **"Our budget can't handle this brand name! Should I buy it anyway?"**

- **"Ugh—should I be worried about that friend?"**

- **"Oh no, I probably need to warn her about this…"**

Parenting can be a noisy environment. Pretty true, isn't it?

MY ACTIVE ZONE:

In KidUnique, we are challenged to "listen" for God's voice concerning our kid. In our noisy worlds, that truly is a challenge. God wants to speak to you about your kid. Today, break through the "noise" of your voice and the noise of your day to ask God two simple questions:

1. "God, is there anything you want to say to me about my kid?"

2. "God, what should I notice today about my kid?"

So, here is the challenge…we each need to shut up and take a walk. Seriously. Find 15-30 minutes today, tonight, or tomorrow morning to just get out of your routine and walk around the block "with" God. Ask the two questions above, listen for any type of heavenly response or thoughts you may have and see what happens.*** If you want to write out some things to remember from the walk, use the space on the next page.

On my walk...

176

***It is possible that you think this is nuts! The concept of "listening" for God's voice may be a totally new concept for you. That is OK, give this a try anyway. Do not be worried, you are not going to hear an audible voice or see bushes catch on fire. This exercise is about quieting yourself and listening. Listen to your heart, to God, and to the quiet. Just keep in mind that God wants to relate to you—be open to that. God longs to speak to you and lead you. Ask him the questions and seek to hear from God.

Here are responses to quiet that you might experience:

A Prompting – When you ask God the two questions, he might answer you with a "prompting." He might prompt some action from you. It might be a message for you to do something (write a note, make a call, have a conversation, issue an apology). Follow up on this and do not ignore it.

New Information/Encouragement – God might open up some new views for you as you listen to his heart concerning your kids. Listen for that. God has a way of bringing a "fresh" look when you give him some space to do so. Take note of any new info on your kid. Remember it and ponder it. God might also let you know that he is proud of you during your little walk. He might bring to mind a story or two when you "did it right." Be ready for that as you listen to him about your kid. God loves to communicate this way to leaders. You, as a KidUnique adult, are a "leader."

Nothing – Nada. Zip. You might not hear God's voice or feel his presence on your walk. This is not uncommon and sometimes it happens. God is not on a vacation in Fiji or too busy for you. For whatever reasons, it is just not happening. Do not worry; just enjoy the walk! Do not give up; try the walk again in a few days.

"Just keep in mind that God wants to relate to you—be open to that. God longs to speak to you and lead you."

REVELATION – Day 3

Get Some Help

Big Idea: *Asking God for what you most want for your kid.*

> *"KidUnique adults believe that God*
>
> *made their kids, knows them better,*
>
> *and loves them deeper than they ever could.*
>
> *KidUnique adults believe that*
>
> *God wants to help with this process."*

KidUnique, page 85

A large part of understanding our roles as KidUnique adults is getting to the point of understanding that a kid ultimately belong to God. Trusting God with our kids is a step of humility and wisdom. Asking for God's help in loving and guiding kids is what the Revelation window is all about.

There is power in reaching out to God in prayer on behalf of our kids. Going to God "with" them through prayer is one of the most influential things we can do as a KidUnique adult. Praying for your kid is a privilege. Praying for your kid is powerful. Would you like to get better at it? Read on...

MY ACTIVE ZONE:

Today, your task will require your best effort. You are going to write out a prayer to God for your kid. This will take some quiet reflection and thought. It might not be easy, but when you're done, you will feel full and free.

On page 92, Dan shares an example of a prayer he wrote. Read through it before you start writing; it will help you. Notice how authentic and real it is. He is just being himself. Make your prayers specific to your kid. Make them come from your heart and direct them to God's heart. Also notice how humble the prayer is. Dan wrote it with an attitude of submission. He wants God's presence and help. Write your prayer with those components: Make it real, make it specific, and ask for help.

Do not put this off! Do it right now. Use this page and get at it! You might want to mark this page and come back to it over and over again. Let it remind you to pray.

Dear God...

_____

_____

_____

_____

_____

_____

_____

_____

_____

_____

_____

_____

Something to think about: **Do you think your parents ever prayed for you?**

REVELATION – Day 4

Real Influence

Big Idea: *Using God's Word to guide your prayers for your kid.*

Here is a story of simple influence...

I have a friend who recently started praying with his sixth-grade son. This routine began during the boy's little league baseball games, sometimes in high-stress situations. Between innings in the dugout or before games in his truck, they will pray for things like confidence and patience. This dad will put his arms on the kid's shoulders and close his eyes and lead his son in a short two- or three-paragraph prayer. When I asked him why he started to do it, his answer was simple. *"I knew we needed more power than I could supply."* This dad and son will for sure find other places to pray together as the kid grows up. How cool is that? How do you think that son feels when his dad steps up like that?

If you are a parent, you are the primary earthly influence on your child. It is your God-given role! No other family member, teacher, neighbor, coach, or friend has the inside edge to influence like you. As a parent, that responsibility is pretty sobering. Truth be told, most of the time, we do not feel up to the challenge, do we? Like the dad in the story you just read, we know that we need "more power" than we can supply. We need God. We need his power. We need to PRAY!

MY ACTIVE ZONE:

Today's exercise will help you to build the skill of prayer into your relationship with your kid. A powerful way to build prayer into your parenting is to pray through passages of God's Word on behalf of your child. Taking significant passages of the Bible and praying through those promises for the people you love is a great skill to build. Can you imagine how much God loves these prayers?

Below are two passages to pray for your kid. Read through them and fill in the blanks with your kid's name. Drink in the words and promises. Bring your requests to God using his Word. Take a few moments and pray these passages today for your kid.

"I ask you God to give _____ a real and clear knowledge of your will

and give _____ spiritual wisdom and understanding.

That way _____'s life will always honor and please you,

and _____'s life will produce every kind of good fruit.

All the while, _____ will grow as

he/she learns to know you better and better.

I also pray that _____ will be strengthened with your glorious power so

he/she will have all the endurance and patience needed.

May _____ be filled with joy, always thanking you.

God, you have enabled _____ to share in the inheritance that belongs to your people,

who live in the light."

Colossians 1:9b-12

"Oh, that _____ might know the joy of those who do not follow the advice of the wicked, or stand around with sinners, or join in with scoffers. May _____ delight in doing everything you want; and may _____ think day and night about your law. Let _____ be like trees planted along the riverbank, bearing fruit each season without fail.

May _____'s leaves never wither, and in all _____ does, let him/her prosper. May _____ not be like the wicked who are worthless chaff that is scattered like the wind."

Psalm 1:1-4

Other passages to pray through:
Jeremiah 29:11-14
John 15:4-11
Ephesians 1:18-19

Take a Walk and Listen – Part 2

Big Idea: *Hearing heaven's thoughts about you.*

I have a friend who has his supervisor on "E-mail Alert." Whenever his boss sends him an e-mail it is automatically marked **"URGENT."** The message shows up in bright red and immediately goes to the top of his inbox. It is a pretty cool feature that most of us have on our e-mail servers, but not many of us use it. My friend uses it because he is determined not to miss a message from his boss.

If we could set the **"Alert...this is a message from God"** buzzer on high, I am guessing most of us would do it. God is a communicator. The Bible talks about the primary ways that he "talks" to us. He uses the Bible and prayer. He will speak through teachers and a community of friends who follow him (the church). He speaks loudly to us through his creation in nature. God is not silent.

Imagine spending some time with God...

What would it be like to actually hang out with God? Maybe you would take God to a favorite place of yours...a great park, a boat dock, your garden, a hilltop. What would your conversation be like? You might have a few questions you would like answered. You might ask about heaven and the afterlife. You might ask about an experience from your past. You might ask about the Chicago Cubs' chances of ever winning a World Series. You might ask him about your kids, like you did a few days ago. You might ask what he was thinking when he made the aardvark.

Once the conversation began to flow and you felt more comfortable, you might even get more personal. What if you asked God this question:

"Is there anything I need to hear from you about me?"

MY ACTIVE ZONE:

So, here's the deal:

Go take another walk. Have the courage to talk with God and ask that question. Give yourself some time; do not be in a hurry. Just linger. Allow God the opportunity to speak to you. Do not make this about KidUnique. Do not make it about work or family or whatever. Just let it be about whatever it is about. Sound too "mystical?" Sound too "out there?" Good. Keep it there and just be with God. Let him speak to you and just listen.

How did it go? What did you hear?

_____

_____

_____

_____

_____

_____

_____

_____

_____

_____

_____

Encouragement – God might let you know that he is proud of you during your little walk. He might bring to mind a story or two when you "did it right." If that kind of conversation happens, enjoy it and don't rush through it!

Rebuke – God might challenge you about something that needs to change in you. On your walk, be ready for things like this. Don't be afraid of it. God is crazy about you, and he disciplines those he loves. God doesn't want to blow you up! He wants to form your heart. Be alert...

Your Family – Because you have spent the last month focused on your kids, this little walk might solidify some of what you've been learning about your family. Let God speak to you about this. Make it personal!

Next Steps – God might want to direct you in a certain way at this stage of your life. Be alert to messages like this:

- "Get some help with that."
- "Apologize to that person."
- "Give this a try."
- "Serve in this ministry."
- "Humble yourself."

Again, don't rush this. Rarely will God set you on a completely new path in your life from a one-hour walk with him. His guidance is often a "process." Let God lead. Fight the temptation to "control" and just follow.

Peace – God might not have a bunch of specific details to impress on you during your walk. He might just lead you to relax and enjoy his presence. If that's the case, and it often is, just experience his peace. Notice nature. Notice people. Notice him.

Don't hurry!

REVELATION – Day 6

Reflection Questions

1. What was the biggest challenge for you as you have attempted to engage God in the process of helping your kid discover who he or she is?

2. What have you learned about listening to God as you engaged the revelation window?

3. What have you learned about yourself as you engaged the revelation window?

4. What was the most significant **message** you heard from God during this last week?

5. What is the **biggest shift** you need to make if you are to continue to consistently look through the Revelation window?

AFFIRMATION – Day 7

"Me in the Mix"

Big Idea: *What I am learning along the way.*

A phrase that best describes my experience with KidUnique this last week is...

Evaluate the five **REVELATION Window** exercises:

Check the ones you did:	Rate the Experiences:
☐ **Day 1 -** GOD SPEAKS—THE "Q"	So-so................pretty good................fantastic
☐ **Day 2 -** TAKE A WALK AND LISTEN PART 1	So-so................pretty good................fantastic
☐ **Day 3 -** GET SOME HELP	So-so................pretty good................fantastic
☐ **Day 4 -** REAL INFLUENCE	So-so................pretty good................fantastic
☐ **Day 5 -** TAKE A WALK AND LISTEN PART 2	So-so................pretty good................fantastic

Which exercise was best and why do you think it worked so well?

What has been happening in you this last week as you have interacted with your kid?

What have you noticed about your relationship with your kid?

Have you received any fresh thoughts from God?

Is there anything that needs changing in you so you can do better at KidUnique?

Is there an issue that has surfaced that you will need to think more about in the future?

PAUSE—Use the space below to record any other thoughts you want to keep track of as you move through the KidUnique experience.

Week 5

The Celebration
Writing a *'WHAT'S RIGHT WITH YOU'* letter

Congratulations on completing the four weeks of exercises applying the four-window model. I hope you have learned as much about yourself as the kid you love. Now you get to finish strong this week by creating a "What's Right With You" letter for your kid.

This letter is a gift you give that blesses and honors your kid. It communicates that you have studied your kid and that he or she is indeed KidUnique. It is something to put on the dresser and look at whenever he or she has doubts about identity. How your letter looks will be determined by the age of your kid and the number of insights you have gleaned concerning him or her over the last month. If your kid is 7 the letter will be shorter and simpler than if he or she is 17.

Dan has already shared with you the letters he wrote to his two older sons Luke and Landan. On the next couple pages you will find the letter Dan wrote to his youngest son, Logan. It can give you a sense of what you might want to create. Consider beginning the letter with a personal word about what your kid means to you. Then be specific about what is right with him or her, listing the characteristics you want to point out. There is room on pages 191-193 for you to work on a draft of your own letter. You will want to work on the letter until you can type it on a single page. Then consider framing the letter making a gift they will remember. Consider giving it to them at a special meal or ceremony. Let your kid know that this is just the beginning of uncovering the truth of who he or she is as a child of God.

> *"This letter is a gift you give that blesses and honors your kid."*

Logan –

Recently I spoke to a group of parents on the topic of parenting. It was intimidating because I often wonder what the heck I know about the topic. There is no question fathering has been one of the best experiences of my life. I have loved being (and still do love being) your dad. I know that there have been times when I've been a good and wise father. And I know that at other times I've angered, frustrated, been stupid, and generally messed up as a dad.

Anyway...I suggested to the moms and dads that they consistently work at reminding their kids what's RIGHT with them instead of always throwing their shortcomings in their face. We each live in our own skin and know where we screw up and fall short. Who needs to be reminded of that, right? As I thought about this I realized that I haven't told you in a while what's RIGHT with you from my perspective.

So, here goes...my reminder of what's RIGHT with you.

First, you are fun loving and enjoy life. I dig this about you. You go for it! You celebrate and enjoy the opportunities life brings and you are fun to be with. God has created an incredible world to enjoy and experience. I know he gets a kick out of watching you live.

Second, you are smart. I know you don't think you are, but you are. Not just because you get good grades. You listen and put things together in your head and figure stuff out. That's smart...and you are that!

Third, you are romantic. Chicks dig romantic...and you have all that. Your heart feels deeply and you enjoy the heartbeat of love. This is an amazing thing for a guy your age. Whoever you marry will be lucky to have you.

Fourth, you are a leader. You don't realize it yet, but I believe that many of your happiest moments in life will come as you are leading something. Logan, it's in you. People take you seriously when you have a passion or cause to move ahead. I know what I'm talking about here. Don't shy back when you get opportunities to lead. God has put this gift into you.

Fifth, you are secure. You walk to the beat of your own drum. In third grade you told three fifth-grade bullies, "Hey, you can't tell me what to do or how to live." Keep saying it Logan. Keep listening to God's voice and following the path he leads you on.

> "Fifth, you are secure. You walk to the beat of your own drum. In third grade you told three fifth-grade bullies, 'Hey, you can't tell me what to do or how to live.'"

Sixth, you are brave. Broken arms, chipped teeth, coming out to take a corner kick, attacking a forward as he approaches the goal on a breakaway. You don't hesitate, you go! It makes sense that the Lord would wrap your heart in bravery. You'll need this for the adventures that are yet ahead of you.

Seventh, you are trustworthy. Your word is your word. Very few men ever get to a place where they can be trusted. You have at a young age. I honor you for this.

Eighth, you have a heart after God. This God loves. To care about how God feels about life is so important. To consider what God might think about something is so rare. Continue to nurture this. Don't ever be embarrassed by it.

God honors those who honor him.

Not bad...eight RIGHT things about Logan: fun loving and enjoys life - smart - romantic - a leader - secure - brave - trustworthy and a heart after God

I celebrate these about you Logan...you should too. Know I love and believe in you son. As always, for you...anything, anytime, anywhere.

Christmas 2003 –

Dad

WHAT'S RIGHT WITH YOU Letter - first draft

WHAT'S RIGHT WITH YOU Letter - first draft

_____

_____

_____

_____

_____

_____

_____

_____

_____

_____

_____

_____

_____

_____

_____

_____

_____

_____

WHAT'S RIGHT WITH YOU Letter - first draft

Now What?

Congratulations on completing the *KidUnique* experience. I am sure you learned as much about yourself as the kid you love. I am also guessing that you have lots of questions concerning where you go from here.

*Concerning continuing to help your kid discover who they are...*as you know, this experience is just one step in a long journey of discovery. Maybe your kid is in elementary school and this experience simply united the two of you. You had the chance to look your kid in the face and connect in new and meaningful ways. If so, I think that is fantastic. Maybe your kid is 17 and this has surfaced the fact that you have some challenges ahead. That is good too. Either way, you are in the game and I applaud that. My hope is that you will never see your kid the same way again. I hope you will be awake to observation, exploration, affirmation, and revelation the rest of your life as you relate to kids.

To continue the journey I want you to know that there are some wonderful resources out there for you to go after. The first is the *KidUnique* website (kidunique.com). Visit us. There you can hear the success stories of others and even share the story of what you are learning with your kid as you continue this journey. You may even have an original exercise that you did with your kid and applies one of the windows. If so, go online and tell us about it.

I want to encourage you to keep reading and growing as an adult who understands and connects with kids. Here are some great books for you to study if you want to go the next step in understanding and helping kids discover who they are:

Disconnected: Parenting Teens in a MySpace World by Chap and Dee Clark

The Element by Ken Robinson

Confident Parenting by Jim Burns

The Truth About You: Your Secret to Success by Marcus Buckingham

*Concerning helping YOU discover who YOU are...*often adults who enter the KidUnique experience rethink their own life. Many admit that they long to have greater clarity as to the life they are meant to life. I am glad this happens. When it does pay attention to the questions it pushes to the surface in your life.

As I mentioned in the **Gratitudes** at the beginning of this book, I facilitate LifePlans for people attempting to live their extraordinary life. Maybe you are at a place of transition or simply longing for more meaning in life. Before you do something drastic, consider investing in yourself by investing in a LifePlan™. LifePlans help an individual refocus their life and set direction for their vocation and personal future. A LifePlan™ is a custom-tailored MasterPlan that defines your "total-life" strategy. It is a charted pathway, inspired by God and careful life process work, leading toward your focused LifeMission.

LifePlans are a one-to-one, two-day process, that I facilitate. I am a Master Level facilitator in the Tom Paterson LifePlan™ process. This proven two-day experience allows the individual to determine and set direction for a personal strategy that results in maximum life impact. The goal of a LifePlan™ is for you to leave both understanding and motivated to live the life you were meant to live. If you are interested in pursuing a LifePlan™, you can learn more at authenticleadershipinc.com.

There is one other suggestion I would like to make if you are sensing a longing to grow personally. Consider working through The REAL DEAL, Becoming More Authentic in Your Life and Leadership. I love helping leaders live into all God has made them to be. This workbook addresses key issues to living fully from who you are, not who others want you to be. My final suggestion has to do with hosting a KidUnique workshop. Information on this exciting opportunity is on the following page.

Available at authenticleadershipinc.com

Dan Webster
Founder
Authentic Leadership, Inc.
550 Old Orchard Road
Holland, MI   49423
616-335-8500

Hosting a **kid**unique workshop

Parents, youth workers and teachers are all concerned for the mental, emotional, physical, and spiritual development of the young. *KidUnique equips those entrusted with the development of the next generation to go one step further and help kids solve the mystery of "me."* Every life is a mystery waiting to be solved, not a mistake needing to be corrected. Entering adulthood with clarity as to who we are and what we are impassioned to do is priceless for a young person. Investing the needed time and energy into this all-important task of helping our kids discover who they are so they can win in life is just plain smart.

This half-day learning experience will equip adults to powerfully impact kids by clarifying the four windows through which we see them and present a simple system for collecting insights that a kid will carry with them into their future.

www.kidunique.com

KidUnique: Helping Kids Discover Who They Are is a wonderful preparative experience for any parent, youth worker, coach, or teacher who cares about investing in kids. This event launches a month-long focus on kids that will generate a lifetime of dialogue leading kids into their future.

The event is best done on a Saturday morning and includes three interactive sessions that incorporate teaching, personal discovery and discussion. This event has a follow-up *31-Day Follow Up Experience* built into it that can be customized to your church, organization, or family.

TAKE AWAY VALUE

Every adult walks away from this experience with:
- *a working knowledge of the four windows through which we watch kids grow and develop*
- *a system for gathering and sharing the core truths that define your kid*
- *a book that is both a guide and journal to track discoveries and insights*
- *a follow-up 31-Day Experience that will lead you to greater levels of skill in helping your kids discover who they are*

Notes

Notes

Notes

Notes